# Ethics

## What We Still Know After a Skeptical Age

## by
## Charles Siegel

Preservation

Aut
facere
scribenda | aut
scribere
legenda

Institute

ISBN 978-0-9788728-3-0
Cover illustration: Poseidon and Apollo from the frieze of the Parthenon.
Published by the Preservation Institute, Berkeley, California.
www.preservenet.com

# Contents

# Chapter 1

# Two Views of Nature

The main classical tradition of ethics is based on the idea of natural flourishing. The nature of an acorn is to grow into an oak tree, and the nature of a baby is to grow into an adult with full human abilities. Gardeners help trees to flourish, to develop their natures fully. The virtues help people to flourish, to develop human nature fully.

This classical tradition in ethics assumes that living things have natural goals, and it was originally based on the view that all of nature was teleological. In Aristotle's *Physics,* inanimate matter has goals, like living things: for example, fire rises upward because its goal is to reach its natural location in the heavens. Matter moves toward its natural goals, just as the acorn grows toward its natural goal of becoming an oak.

This teleological view of nature was exploded in the seventeenth century, when the new physics of Galileo and Newton showed that the motion of matter is caused by forces that act on it, not by its natural goals. Because they believed that all nature is composed of matter in motion, many seventeenth and eighteenth century philosophers thought the new physics could also explain the behavior of living things. Some philosophers, such as Descartes, believed that we could explain the behavior of plants and animals in purely mechanical terms, but that humans had a soul with free will which was not controlled by mechanical causes. Other philosophers, such as La Mettrie, believed that we could also explain human behavior in purely mechanical terms.

By destroying the teleological view of nature, the new physics undermined classical ethics. The final causes of Aristotle, natural goals at which things aimed, were replaced by the efficient causes of the new physics, forces that caused matter to move. Matter had no inherent goals, and because living things are made of matter, living things also had no inherent goals. Philosophers tried to create new ethical theories that were compatible with this new view of nature, but as we will see, they failed to create a firm foundation for ethics.

The new physics helped pave the way for the industrial revolution by making it possible to develop technologies that manipulate matter. And if living things – plants, animals and, if you do not believe in the soul, also humans – are nothing more than complex arrangements of matter, with no inherent ends of their own, then you can manipulate living things as you manipulate other resources used by the industrial economy.

This ideology was useful from the seventeenth century through the early twentieth century, at a time when the West needed to abandon scruples that stopped it from unleashing modernization, in order to overcome scarcity.

But today, we need to control modernization, to subordinate modernization to human values. At a time when it has become clear that the earth cannot support endless economic growth, we need to be able to decide when we already have enough to live a good life. At a time when some scientists are claiming that they will soon "improve" humans through genetic engineering, we need to respect human nature enough to limit bio-technologies. We need to modernize selectively, using technologies that enhance our lives and limiting technologies that are destructive.

Reviving the main classical tradition of ethics, based on nature and on human nature, can let us move beyond the ethical theories of the age of modernization and can make it clear that we should modernize in ways that serve the goal of natural flourishing.

This classical ethical theory is usually called "natural law," but this term is misleading. It implies that nature somehow has laws like the laws in the law books, so it also implies that there must be a Law Giver, putting off many people by bringing in religious issues that are not necessary to this theory of ethics.

"Natural law" is actually a bad translation of the Latin "*jus naturale*." The English word "law" usually has the meaning of the Latin word "*lex*," a law enacted by the state. The Latin word "*jus*" sometimes is used to mean a law that is based on usage or custom and has not been enacted formally by the state, but it is also used to mean "right" or "justice" – and *jus naturale* seems to have this second meaning, that certain acts are wrong because they are in conflict with nature. Instead of "natural law," *jus naturale* should be translated as "natural morality" or "natural ethics."

# Chapter 2

# Natural Ethics

The central classical tradition in ethics says that natural goods, such as health, strength and knowledge, are self-evidently good. Moral goods – virtues – are habits that help us to attain these natural goods. But virtues are not just means to natural goods: the moral capability itself, the ability to understand what is right and to act on this understanding, is also an important part of human nature, so the virtues themselves are natural goods. In addition to being means to the end of attaining natural goods, the virtues are ends in themselves – and, in fact, are central to living a good life.

In this chapter, we will sketch a theory of ethics based on our intuitive conviction that natural goods are, in fact, good. In later chapters, we will look at why modern philosophers were wrong to reject classical ethics, and we will develop a more rigorous basis for classical ethics, but these later chapters will be clearer if we begin by sketching a theory of classical natural ethics that seems intuitively convincing. We will look only at natural goods and will ignore the theological overlay that is often included in theories of natural ethics, in order to develop a view of ethics that is still convincing today, after a skeptical age.

## Natural Goods

The most obvious of the natural goods is health. Everyone sees that it is bad to be unhealthy. For example, if you break your leg and cannot walk, or if you have a bad case of the flu and can hardly get out of bed, it is obvious that something is wrong with your body.

Though health is the most obvious, there are many other natural goods that everyone recognizes. Strength is one: when people try to lift things, we can see that someone who is strong does it well, but someone who is weak does it badly or cannot do it at all. Intelligence is another: when people try to learn mathematics, for example, we can see that someone who is intelligent can understand the lessons well, but someone who is stupid cannot understand them completely. Just as we see that health is good and illness is bad, we see that strength is good and weakness is bad, that intelligence is good and stupidity is bad, and so on.

These natural goods are all are a matter of some natural capability functioning well.

Health involves the body functioning well in basic ways. For example, our lungs have the function of breathing. Our lungs are healthy if they perform this basic function well and are diseased if they do not perform this basic function well. We consider asthma and emphysema diseases precisely because the lungs are not performing their natural function well.

Other natural goods are a matter of other capabilities functioning well. People are strong if their muscles function well and weak if their muscles function badly. People are intelligent if their intellects function well and stupid if their intellects function badly. Notice that physical strength goes beyond the base-line functioning required for health: if someone's muscles are paralyzed or atrophied, we consider that person unhealthy, but if someone's muscles are not strong enough to lift 150 pounds, we do not consider that person unhealthy, just weaker than someone who can lift the weight.

The idea that our capabilities function well or badly depends on the idea that these capabilities have inherent functions or purposes.

For example, the function of your muscles is to move your body or to move objects: if you are strong enough to lift heavy weights, your muscles are performing this function well, but if you are too weak to lift weights, your muscles are not performing this function well.

The function of your eyes is to see things; if you see clearly, your eyes function well, but if you cannot see the book in front of you clearly enough to read it, or if you cannot see someone a few yards away clearly enough to recognize him, then your eyes do not function well.

The function of your intellect is to understand ideas: if you understand complex ideas easily, your intellect functions well, and if you cannot understand simple ideas, your intellect does not function well.

In other words, these natural goods all depend on natural teleology – on the inherent purposes of our natural capabilities. Everyone knows this, though most people cannot put it into words. For example, everyone knows that it is good to have 20-20 vision, and that it is bad to be nearsighted or blind because the function of the eyes is to see things, which implies that it is good for them to see things well, bad for them to see things unclearly, and worse for them not to be able to see at all.

# Moral Goods

Moral goods (or virtues) are habits that help us to attain these natural goods. There are two broad classes of virtues: those that bring natural goods to oneself and those that bring natural goods to others.

### Virtues Aimed at Yourself

Of the traditional four cardinal virtues – temperance, fortitude, prudence, and justice – the first three help to bring natural goods to yourself. In other words, they help you to live successfully.

Temperance is necessary to protect your health. Eating excessively makes you obese, and drinking excessively weakens your body and dulls your mind.

Fortitude (or perseverance) is necessary to succeed at most anything you try to accomplish. To build up your physical strength, you must keep exercising, not give up as soon as you start getting tired. To become knowledgeable, you must keep studying and not give up as soon as it becomes hard to understand the subject. To succeed at most things, you must keep trying and not be discouraged by one or two failures.

Prudence also is necessary to succeed at most anything. You have to think about the long-term effects of your decisions, rather than just doing what appeals to you at the moment, in order to make good decisions and succeed at most things you try to accomplish.

We could easily expand the list by adding other virtues that are necessary to live successfully, such as patience and diligence.

There are vices that correspond to these virtues. Gluttony and other forms of over-indulgence are the opposites of temperance. Fecklessness and giving up easily are the opposites of fortitude. Impulsiveness and foolishness are the opposites of prudence. Laziness is the opposite of diligence. All of these vices should be avoided, because they prevent you from living successfully.

These virtues are not self-evidently good in the same way that natural goods are. Everyone (even children) can see that it is good to be healthy, strong, and so on, but some people (particularly children and adolescents) do not see that it is good to be temperate and prudent.

We learn about the moral goods from experience. We recognize that they are virtues or vices because we have seen over and over again that spending your life drinking destroys your health, that diligence helps you to succeed at most tasks, and so on.

These virtues let both individuals and groups of people live successfully: for example, prudence is important in personal decisions, and is also important in political decisions.

## Virtues Aimed at Others

There are also virtues that help bring natural goods to others. Of the traditional cardinal virtues, justice is the one that is aimed at others' well-being. We can easily create a list of virtues aimed at others' well-being by adding charity, honesty, loyalty, and so on.

There are also vices that are the opposite of these virtues. For example, stealing, cheating, and lying are wrong because they are ways of manipulating other people for your own purposes, without thinking about what is good for them.

If we consider when it is wrong to lie, we can see that these vices are wrong because they sacrifice the good of others to your own good. It is clearly wrong to lie in order to benefit yourself at the expense of another person: for example, it is wrong for a building inspector to lie and say a house has termites so he can buy the house at a bargain price and resell it at a profit. But it is not necessarily wrong to tell a "white lie" to benefit another person: if a doctor finds that someone has a 50-50 chance of living but that he is much more likely to recover if he is optimistic about his chances, then it would not be wrong for the doctor to tell the person that he has a good chance of recovering.

Most of the virtues aimed at the good of others involve general obligations to all people, but we also have special obligations to certain people. For example, because children are emotionally damaged if they are abandoned by their parents, we have a special obligation to our own children: as their parents, we are the ones who can give them the stable family that helps them develop well.

The virtues directed at others are all based on the insight that the natural goods of other people are as important as one's own natural goods. The statements that health is good, that knowledge is good – and more generally that it is good for any natural capability to function well – are true of everyone: they are as true of others as they are of oneself. We have an emotional bias toward ourselves, an impulse to pursue our own goods even at the expense of others, but if we step back and look at things more dispassionately, we see that other people have the same nature that we do. If it is good for me to realize my nature fully, it is also good for other people to realize their natures fully.

10

As a practical matter, we can usually do more to promote our own good than to promote the goods of others: I can exercise to build my own strength, and I can study to build my own knowledge, but I cannot do the work of exercising and studying for other people. But it is good to help others, and it is wrong to sacrifice another person's good to promote your own good – for example, by stealing.

## Moral Capability as a Natural Good

The virtues are means to natural goods, but they are not important only as a means. They are also ends in themselves.

The ability to judge right from wrong and the ability to conform our actions to this judgment, are part of human nature, like the ability to speak or to walk. It is good for these capabilities to function well, just as it is for any human capability to function well.

In fact, most people would consider it much worse to lack a moral sense than to lack physical strength, musical ability, or most other natural goods. If someone cannot see that it is wrong to habitually get so drunk that you cannot think straight, or cannot see that it is wrong to murder or torture other people, we would consider him a monster – much worse than someone who is physically weak or who lacks musical talent.

Likewise, most people would also consider it much worse to lack the ability control your actions so they conform to your moral judgment than it is to lack other natural goods. If someone knows that it is destructive to be chronically drunk but cannot stop drinking, or knows that it is unhealthy to be obese but cannot stop overeating, we would feel sorry for him – not just because he is damaging his health, but because his weak character itself is pitiful.

On the other hand, if someone is crippled or blind and has the strength of character to be successful, most of us would admire her for overcoming those handicaps. We consider the strong character that she has more important than physical capabilities that she lacks.

This shows that most people think our moral capability is the most important of our natural capabilities, that it is central to living a good life, as the main tradition of classical philosophy said.

Though we have an intuitive sense that these moral capabilities are more important than other human capabilities, it is hard to see clearly why they are more important. In warlike nomadic societies, most people would say that physical strength is more important. It hard to come up with an absolutely clear reason for deciding which of our capabilities are more important than others – even though we have a strong subjective feeling that these moral capabilities are essential to our humanity.

By contrast, we can see absolutely clearly that it is good for any of our natural capabilities – including these moral capabilities – to function well. It is absolutely clear that it is good to be healthy and bad to be sick, good to be able to keep your resolutions and bad to habitually fail at keeping your resolutions, and so on.

As Alasdair McIntyre has said, this classical ethical theory is teleological without being consequentialist. It is teleological because the virtues are means to the good life – for oneself and others. But it is not consequentialist because the virtues are not merely means, which have no importance in themselves. The virtues themselves are also an important part of the good life.

# Arete

The main tradition of classical ethics is based on our intuitive certainty that it is good for our natural capabilities to function well – good to breathe normally and bad to have emphysema, good to be intelligent and bad to be stupid, and so on – but we have no word in English meaning that all natural capabilities are all functioning well. Our word "health" means that the basic physical capabilities are functioning well, but there is no equivalent word for all the human capabilities – no word to describe someone whose health, intelligence, musical talent, moral capability, and other capabilities are all functioning well.

The Greek word "arete" has this meaning, and it was central to classical ethics. It is usually translated as "virtue," but translators often explain that really means something more like excellence. It includes not only the moral virtues but also every other sort of excellence. As we use the English word "virtue," someone has virtue if he is morally good, no matter how unhealthy or weak or untalented he is. But someone has arete only if he is living a good life overall.

Though we do not have a word for it, most everyone can see the value of arete. One person is healthy, strong, intelligent, honest, a devoted parent, and a skilled worker. Another person spends all day drinking beer and chain smoking cigarettes, has a chronic cough and slurred speech, abandoned his children, and supports himself though petty theft. Everyone can see that the first person is living a better life than the second person. Everyone will respect the first person and feel pity or contempt for the second person.

## The Limits of Arete

The ideal of arete, as it has been sketched here, cannot give us a complete theory of ethics for two reasons.

First, the ideal of arete does not tell us how to balance our own good against the good of others. It is clear that we should not ignore the good of others completely, as (for example) slave owners and thieves do. But it also seems plausible that we should not give the good of others equal weight with our own good, since this would prevent us from developing most of our talents. If I gave equal weight to my own good and others' good, I would spend all my time earning money to buy food for people who are dying because of famine in the poorest parts of the world. But if I worked one hundred hours a week to make money to donate to the poor, I would not have any free time to practice music, exercise physically, read books, or develop my other talents. Of course, if my own children were starving, I would be willing to work every moment of the day to buy them food, but there does not seem to be any way to balance the urgent needs of all the poor people in the world with our desire to develop our own talents. At least, the idea of arete does not give us an easy answer to this question.

Second, the ideal of arete, as it has been sketched here, does not tell us which human capabilities are most important. Because we have a limited amount of time, we must choose which of our capabilities to develop: we cannot spend enough time exercising to develop our bodies to their utmost, and also spend enough time studying to develop our minds to their utmost, and also spend enough time playing instruments to develop our musical abilities to their utmost, and also spend enough time helping other people to develop our charitable virtue to its utmost, and so on. These goods make conflicting claims on our time, so we must choose among them, but the theory we have sketched in this chapter does not help us rank the goods and decide which to choose.

There are two obvious possibilities for allocating our time among the goods. One is to try to be well rounded, focusing on developing all your capabilities. The other is to try to specialize, focusing on developing one capability where you have the most talent. The idea of arete alone does not tell us which of these to choose.

To know which human capabilities are most important, we have to know the overall purpose of human life. If Catholics are right to believe that the purpose of life is salvation, then all the other capabilities are important in so far as they serve this purpose. If Hindus are right to believe that the purpose of life is union with Brahman through yoga and meditation, then all the other capabilities are important in so far as they serve this purpose. Aristotle believed that intellectual contemplation and moral virtue were our highest most divine capabilities, and that even though we are human, we should do as much as we can to elevate ourselves to the level of the divine by developing these capabilities: this was his view of the overall purpose of human life.

It is plausible that some human capabilities are higher than others in some way, as Aristotle believed. It is also plausible that human life is higher than animal life in some way, and that animal life is higher than plant life in some way. Yet these things are not absolutely clear, as it is clear that it is good for any natural capability to function well. When Aristotle talks about our highest and most divine capabilities, he is moving from natural ethics, which we can understand clearly, to theology, which we cannot understand as clearly.

The overall purpose of human life is certainly not self-evident, so an ethical theory based on arete does not tell us, by itself, which natural capabilities are most important.

**The Uses of Arete**

Despite these limits, the ideal of arete can give us real ethical guidance.

This ideal gives us some positive guidance. We can see that positive virtues such as diligence, prudence, and perseverance are necessary to accomplish virtually anything, no matter what is the purpose of life. And we can see that it is good to help other people to survive if their lives are threatened, because survival is necessary to achieve any purpose of life.

This ideal gives us very clear negative guidance. It obviously does not help you achieve any purpose of life if you are gluttonous, habitually drunk, impulsive, or so easily discouraged that you give up the first time you hit an obstacle. And it is obviously does not help other people to achieve any purpose of life if you murder them, exploit them, or prevent them in some other way from exercising their natural capabilities.

For example, many societies have not educated women or given them the right to own property or to vote, and this is obviously wrong because it prevents women from developing their intellectual and moral capabilities. Likewise, it was obviously wrong for slave-owners to illegalize the education of slaves and to turn slaves into property with no right to make decisions about their own lives, because it prevented the slaves from developing their intellectual and moral capabilities.

The history of abolitionism and feminism show that natural ethics makes it possible to criticize the ethics of your own society, because it is independent of any culture's values. Abolitionists, feminists, and the civil rights movement actually did use the principles of natural ethics to argue against oppression and injustice. For example, Martin Luther King used this ethical tradition in his famous "Letter from a Birmingham Jail" to explain why he had broken the law:

> one has a moral responsibility to disobey unjust laws. … An unjust law is a code that is out of harmony with the moral law. To put it in the terms of St. Thomas Aquinas: An unjust law is a human law that is not rooted in eternal law and natural law.[1]

# Chapter 3

# Rejecting Classical Ethics

During much of the history of philosophy, from Aristotle, to the stoics, to the Thomists, most philosophers would have agreed that that ethics is based on nature – that virtues allow human nature to flourish and vices prevent human nature from flourishing. Some schools differed. Platonists were more high-minded and believed that ethics was based on direct knowledge of the transcendent idea of the good. The Epicureans were more low-minded and believed that ethics was based on seeking pleasure and avoiding pain. But the mainstream of philosophy believed ethics was based on nature.

Beginning in the seventeenth century, though, most philosophers rejected this classical view because they rejected Aristotle's teleological view of nature. They tried to develop new ethical theories that were compatible with the new physics of Galileo and Newton, and we will see that they failed.

The most important obstacle to developing a new theory of ethics was a logical principle which was introduced at the time of Hume and Kant and which became central to modern ethical theory. This principle is stated in several ways: it is impossible to derive values from facts, it is impossible to derive normative statements from factual statements, or it is impossible to derive "ought statements" from "is statements."

According to this principle, "ought statements" and "is statements" are logically different, so one cannot imply the other. We cannot reach conclusions about what is by reasoning about what ought to be. Likewise, we cannot reach conclusions about what ought to be by reasoning about what is.

David Hume was the first to state this principle:

In every system of morality, which I have hitherto met with, I have always remarked that the author proceeds for some time in the ordinary way of reasoning, and establishes the being of a God, or makes observations concerning human affairs; when of a sudden I am surprised to find that instead of the usual copulation of propositions, *is*, and *is not*, I meet with no proposition that is not connected with an *ought* or an *ought not*. This change is imperceptible; but is, however, of the last consequence. For as this *ought*, or *ought not*, expresses some new relation or affirmation, it is necessary that it should be observed and explained; and at the same time that a reason should be given, for what seems altogether unconceivable, how this new relation can be a deduction from others, which are entirely different from it.[2]

This principle is sometimes called "Hume's Guillotine," because it severs "ought statements" from "is statements" completely.

This principle meant the end of classical ethics, because it made it impossible to base an ethical theory (what ought to be) on human nature (what is).

# Aristotle

Aristotle based both his physics and his ethics on a teleological view of nature.

If we are pushing a stone along the ground, we must keep applying force to it or it will stop moving, but if we drop a stone, it will move downward without any effort on our part. Why do stones move downward spontaneously, while they resist being moved in other ways? According to Aristotle, it is because they have a tendency to move toward their natural location.

Plants' leaves move toward the sun and their roots seek water because they have a tendency to actualize their nature. Likewise, stones fall and fire rises, Aristotle believed, because they have a tendency to actualize their natures by moving toward their natural location on the earth (for stones) and in the heaven (for fire).

Today we think of physics as the study of inanimate matter, but our word "physics" comes from the Greek word *phusis*, meaning nature. Aristotle's physics was based primarily on observation of living things, which make up most of the nature that we see around us, and he assumed the behavior of inanimate matter is similar to the behavior of living things.

Because he had this teleological view of nature, Aristotle meant something very different from what we mean today when he talked about "natural" behavior. We use the word "natural" to describe the way something actually behaves in nature, but Aristotle used this word to describe behavior that is in keeping with something's natural ends.

For example, Aristotle said "man is by nature a political animal"[3] – meaning that it is natural for people to live in a *polis* (a city-state) because this way of life lets people develop their human capabilities completely. He knew that this is not the way that things actually are in nature: in his time, most people were barbarians who did not live in any civil society at all or who lived in despotic empires, and only a small minority lived in city-states. But Aristotle did not think that the way barbarians lived was natural because it did not let them fully develop their ability to reason, their ability to govern themselves, and other important natural capabilities.

Barbarians were like trees planted in bad soil, which cannot grow naturally. As we usually use the word "natural" today, to mean the way things actually are, we would have to say that it is more natural for an acorn to die or produce a stunted oak tree than it is for the acorn to fall in good soil, get enough water and sunshine, and grow into a healthy oak tree. As things actually behave in nature, most acorns die or are stunted, and only a very few grow to healthy oaks. But as Aristotle used the word "natural," the stunted oak tree is unnatural, because it never fully actualizes its natural potential.

Moving beyond physics to ethics, Aristotle asked which human potentials were most important and should be the focus of a good life. He concluded that intellectual contemplation and, to a lesser extent, moral virtue are the most important human activities.

In one place, he defends this idea on the grounds that rational activity distinguishes people from plants and animals, so they define the essence of what it means to be human. [4] But this argument does not hold up: distinguishing characteristics are not necessarily the essential or most important characteristics. For example, a pick-up truck is distinguished from other motor vehicles because it has a bed to carry cargo, but we would not say that it is a good pick-up truck if it has a beautifully designed bed but a weak engine that stalls out whenever it tries to carry a heavy load. Even though the engine is not a feature that distinguishes pick-up trucks from other motor vehicles, the engine is essential for the pick-up truck to perform its function of hauling things, and a good pick-up truck must have a strong, reliable engine. We have to know the purpose of a pick-up truck (not what distinguishes pick-up trucks from other vehicles) in order to decide what is a good pick-up truck. Likewise, we have to know the purpose of human life (not what distinguishes humans from other animals) in order to decide what is a good human life.

Elsewhere, Aristotle argued that intellectual contemplation was the highest human activity because man can live a life of contemplation "in so far as something divine is present in him" – Aristotle's God is devoted solely to intellectual contemplation – and "we must not follow those who advise, being men, to think of human things ..., but must, so far as we can, make ourselves immortal, and strain with every nerve to live in accordance with the best thing in us. ... And this would seem actually to be each man, since it is the authoritative and better part of him."[5] This idea may also have been in the back of his mind when he said contemplation and virtue were important because they distinguish humans from other animals: not just that they were the distinguishing attribute but also that they were the divine part of our nature, rather than the animal part.

But here Aristotle is moving beyond natural ethics to theology. We can see very clearly that it is good to be healthy and bad to be unhealthy, good to be knowledgeable and bad to be ignorant, and so on. We cannot see as clearly what is the nature of God or what is the relation between our divine and animal nature, so Aristotle's claim that intellectual and moral activity are the highest faculties goes beyond the purely natural ethics sketched in Chapter 2.

# The Stoics

Aristotle believed that natural goods are an important part of the good life: to devote your life successfully to intellectual and moral activity, you must have health, intelligence, education, some wealth, and the like. This means that living a good life is in part a matter of good fortune. If you are extremely poor, unhealthy, or uneducated, you cannot live a fully good life.

The stoics believed, like Aristotle, that the virtues are means to natural goods, such as life, health, and strength. As in the ethical theory we sketched in Chapter 2, the moral goods (or virtues) aim at the natural goods.[6]

However, the stoics' main goal was to achieve tranquility by proving that people have complete control over their ability to live a good life. Therefore, they claimed that virtue was the only good, and the wise man who was completely virtuous was living a supremely good life whatever his external circumstances. Even as he watched his family being murdered, or even as he was being tortured on the rack, a wise man who was completely virtuous was living a supremely good life.

Unlike Aristotle, the stoics were determined to believe that good fortune was not needed to live a good life, and this distorted their ethical theory. Because they could not admit that any good was outside of our own control, they claimed that only the virtues were good, and they called the natural goods "preferred indifferents." They are "preferred" because they are the goals that the virtues aim at, but they are "indifferents" rather than goods, because you can live a supremely good life without them.

The term "preferred indifferents" seems self-contradictory, and there is a real contradiction involved. The goal of the virtues is to attain these natural goods, but the stoics' theory implies that it is just as good to fail at your goal as it is to achieve your goal, as long as you remain virtuous. For example, if you exercise the virtue of temperance in order to protect your health, but through no fault of your own, you catch a contagious disease that makes you an invalid, you are doing just as well as if you had successfully protected your health. If you exercise virtue by bringing food to people who are starving but you are too late and they die before you arrive, you are doing just as well as someone who gets there with food on time and saves their lives.

The stoics were pantheists. They believed that nature as a whole is good, and they thought of nature as providence: whatever demand nature makes of you is the demand of providence, and you should meet it with equanimity as an opportunity that providence has given you to exercise virtue.[7] This pantheism obviously helped them reach their goal of achieving tranquility.

But this pantheism made them confuse the meaning of the word nature. On the one hand, they believed the goal of the virtues was proper functioning of human nature, and here they used the word nature in Aristotle's teleological sense. On the other hand, they believed that nature as a whole is good, using nature in our modern sense to mean the way that things actually happen.

This confusion prevented them from seeing that nature as a whole does not let every person's nature flourish. Just as many acorns never grow into oaks, many people do not actualize their human nature: they die as infants, or they suffer from illness or dementia, or they are thwarted by poverty.

When we look at nature as a whole, we see that often one living thing tries to flourish according to its nature by preventing other living things from flourishing according to their nature: vines overgrow and kill trees, predators kill prey, bacteria cause diseases. Even if we ignore natural goods and care only about moral goods, as the stoics did, we still see that nature as a whole can make it impossible to exercise virtue: many people die as infants before they are capable of exercising any virtues, and some people suffer from brain diseases that prevent them from exercising any virtues.

To think clearly about what it means to act according to nature, we have to make the distinction that the stoics slurred over. It is good for each living thing to flourish according to its nature, and so it follows that nature as a whole is not entirely good.

# The Thomists

Thomas Aquinas revived Aristotle's thinking and integrated it with Catholic doctrine.

He adopted Aristotle's teleological view of nature and used it as the basis of his theory of natural ethics. Everything has a natural end, even inanimate objects: as he said "on the basis of its form, fire, for instance, is inclined toward a higher place, and toward generating its like."[8] Inanimate objects, plants, animals, and humans all have this tendency to move toward their natural end. Dante, who was a Thomist, states this view of nature beautifully when he compares the human soul with inanimate matter:

> … just as fire yearns upward through the air,
> being so formed that it aspires by nature
> to be in its own element up there;
> so love, which is a spiritual motion,
> fills the trapped soul, and it can never rest
> short of the thing that fills it with devotion.[9]

Aquinas said that animals are moved toward their natural ends by their appetites, emotions, and other sensual passions. But humans are moved toward their natural ends by reason as well as by sensual passions: a human does not act directly on passion, as an animal does, "but waits for the command of will, which is the higher appetite."[10] We actively will our actions, and our wills are controlled by our reason as well as by our appetites.

Virtues, for Aquinas as for Aristotle, are habits that allow our reason to harness our passions so we can we can achieve the natural ends of human life more effectively. This is clear if we look at the cardinal virtues: temperance involves reason's ability to control excessive appetites; fortitude involves reason's ability to act despite emotions such as fear or disappointment; justice involves reason's ability to control our impulse toward selfishness in our relations with others; prudence involves being governed by reason generally, rather than acting immediately on passion.

These cardinal virtues were known to the pagans, since they are clearly necessary to live a good life. By contrast, Aquinas said, the theological virtues of faith, hope, and charity are gifts of God and were unknown to the pagans. These theological virtues are needed to achieve the true end of human nature, the beatific vision, the direct, blissful knowledge of God after our deaths, which brings the soul perfect knowledge and understanding.

For Thomists, as for Aristotle, ethics is based on the virtues that allow us to actualize our capabilities fully. But Thomists believe that pagans like Aristotle were not aware of the most important capability of human nature – the capability of theological salvation.

Like Aristotle and others in the main classical tradition, the Thomists believe that virtues are means to natural goods and are also good in themselves, and that the the virtues are the most important goods. It is easy to see why Christians believe this: for example, they think you should feed the hungry to help preserve their health, a natural good, but they also think the virtue of feeding the hungry helps lead you to eternal salvation, which is far more important than worldly goods such as health.

Though Aquinas had a Christian view of the highest end of human nature, he used reason and observation of human nature (not revelation and divine commandment) as the basis of his fundamental ethical idea that virtues are habits that allow human nature to flourish. Thomists today still believe that we can understand this natural law by reason, apart from revelation.

Today's Thomists still say that the goal of their natural ethics is "human flourishing" – letting human nature develop fully in keeping with its natural goals.

# Looking Back at Classical Ethics

The ethical ideas of the classical philosophers were distorted by self-interest or by dogma. Aristotle believed that slavery was natural, because he was protecting his interest as an aristocratic slave owner. The stoics believed that natural goods were not actually goods, because of their dogma that we could control our own happiness and could avoid being affected by changes of fortune.

The classical philosophers did not separate ethics from theology. Aristotle said we should live a life of contemplation and virtue in order to imitate the divine. The stoics said we should submit to nature as providence. Aquinas said that salvation is the central end of human life. These are all theological ideas that we cannot know with the same clarity that we know the basic principles of natural ethics.

Despite the distortions and the theology, this main tradition of moral philosophy, from Aristotle and the stoics to the Thomists, was rooted in a theory of natural ethics that could have developed into a theory like the one sketched in Chapter 2. Yet mainstream philosophy simply scrapped these classical theories of ethics in the seventeenth century, rather than criticizing and refining them.

The theory sketched in this book is more modest than these classical theories. We know with intuitive certainty that health, knowledge, and other forms of human flourishing are good, but we do not know the ultimate good, the overall purpose of life with the same certainty. This book bases ethics on the natural goods that we can understand clearly, natural goods that involve specific capabilities with obvious inherent teleologies, such as the ability of our eyes to see, the ability of our lungs to breathe, and the ability of our minds to understand. This book does not go further by claiming to understand the telos of human life as a whole, or to understand the universe as a whole.

The stripped-down theory of natural ethics sketched in this book is obviously not the whole truth, but it is the part of the truth that we can see clearly, even after a skeptical age.

# The Dilemma of Modernist Ethics

Classical philosophers could base ethics on human nature because they had a teleological view of nature. But scientific discoveries, beginning with the physics of Galileo and Newton, seemed so impressive that modern philosophers tried to explain nature completely based on this new science. In the seventeenth century, philosophers rejected the older teleological view of nature, based on final causes, in favor of the new physics, based solely on prior causes.

Philosophers tried to develop ethical theories based on this new science and on reason, but they failed precisely because they rejected the teleological view of nature. If you ignore final causes and think only in terms of prior causes, you no longer have a basis for the most obvious evaluative conclusions.

The history of moral philosophy since the seventeenth century is the story of a series of failed attempts to get around this problem, as Alasdair MacIntyre has shown.[11]

The next two chapters will look at how modern moral philosophy was stymied by "Hume's Guillotine" – the logical principle that you cannot derive normative statements from factual statements, which means that you cannot base ethics on human nature. This principle led modern ethical theory to develop two major traditions, which both failed to establish an ethical theory that replaced natural ethics.

The first tradition is empiricism, which focuses on factual statements and ultimately fails to derive normative statements from them. It looks at people's actual desires and how they can be satisfied, or it looks at the actual sentiments that are the basis of people's moral judgments, and it tries to use these factual observations as the basis of ethics. These theories seemed plausible when people shared similar desires and moral sentiments, but they failed in the twentieth century, when the moral consensus broke down. Because empiricism is based on observations of people's desires or moral sentiments, it has no way to resolve radical disagreements about ethics by saying that we ought to hold one set of desires or moral sentiments rather than another.

The second tradition is rationalism, which tries to derive normative statements from reason alone, without basing them on observations of human nature. Rationalists try to base ethics on our direct, rational knowledge that some things are good and others are bad. They fail because their principles tend to be vacuous – they do not say enough to tell us what a good life is – and because they cannot answer someone who disagrees and claims to have direct rational knowledge of different moral principles.

Both of these schools founder on the logical difficulty that has dominated philosophers' debates about ethics since the days of Hume and Kant, the idea that we cannot derive normative conclusions from factual premises. If this idea is true, then we cannot base an ethical system on human nature, as classical moral philosophy did. The only alternatives are empiricism, which talks about what actually is and cannot draw conclusions about what they ought to be, and rationalism, which talks about what ought to be without basing its theories on what actually is.

We will see that both of these alternatives failed. As a result, there is no widely accepted modern tradition of moral philosophy that replaced the widely accepted classical tradition of natural ethics.

# Chapter 4

# Modernist Ethics: Empiricism

Empiricists base their ethical theories on observations of people's actual moral judgments and of the motivations behind these judgments.

Early empiricists assumed that moral sentiments were the same everywhere, and that philosophers just had to analyze these common moral sentiments in order to find the basis of ethics. This assumption seemed plausible in Britain between the seventeenth and the nineteenth century, in an insular society where people were complacent about their vision of the good life.

But this assumption no longer seemed plausible in the twentieth century, when anthropologists were describing societies with many different moral systems, and when Europe's own values were being challenged.

During the twentieth century, empiricism turned into moral relativism. Instead of believing that you could base an ethical theory on the sentiments that underlie our common moral judgments, philosophers in the empiricist tradition began to say that value judgments were "merely" expressions of sentiment, that they had no objective validity at all.

## Hobbes' Egoism

In the seventeenth century, Thomas Hobbes developed the first important modern empiricist ethical theory. His theory is often called egoism, because it is based on the idea that people are motivated solely by their own appetites and aversions. It could also be called a type of hedonism, because it is based on the idea that people seek pleasure and avoid pain.

Hobbes rejected the scholasticism that he had been taught in school and its Thomist ethics, he admired the new physics of Galileo, and he tried to develop a scientific theory of ethics and politics. His most important book, *Leviathan*, begins with a section "Of Man" and continues with a section "Of Common-wealth," which describes a well ordered state. But Hobbes originally planned a book that began with a section "Of Body," about the new physics, and then continued with "Of Man" and "Of the Citizen."[12] This initial plan was based on his idea that physics could be the basis of moral and political theory.

Hobbes explained human behavior based on the physics of his time. Motion of matter outside of our bodies affects our senses, which causes motion of matter inside our bodies, which causes our feelings of appetite or aversion, which cause us to seek or to avoid things around us. Our behavior is based on this chain of physical causes.

According to Hobbes, political and ethical philosophy should consist of maxims that help people gratify their feelings of appetite and aversion. In the state of nature before government is formed, he believed, there is a constant war of each against all, as people pursue their own gratification in any way they can. As a result, life in the state of nature is "nasty, brutish and short." In order to gratify themselves more effectively, people agree to a "social contract," creating a government that prevents them from harming one another and that gives the sovereign power to keep the peace.[13]

In this view, self-interest is the basis of all morality. We value the virtues and condemn the vices because they let us live comfortably:

> ... Morall Philosophy is nothing else but the Science of what is *Good* and *Evill*, in the conversation, and Society of mankind. *Good*, and *Evill*, are names that signifie our Appetites, and Aversions ... and consequently all men agree on this, that Peace is Good, and that therefore also the way, or means of Peace, which (as I have shown before) are *Justice, Gratitude, Modesty, Equity,* & the rest of the Laws of Nature, are good; that is to say, *Morall Vertues*; and their contrarie *Vices*, Evill.[14]

Hobbes called his maxims "laws of nature," using the old scholastic language, but after listing the maxims, he admitted that the word "laws" was not really right:

> ... These dictates of Reason, men use to call by the name of Lawes; but improperly: for they are but Conclusions or Theorems concerning what conduceth to the conservation and defence of themselves....[15]

In other words, these principles are just the most effective means of gratifying human appetites and aversions.

The free-market economists who became so influential in England in the centuries after Hobbes wrote also believed that people are motivated by self-interest, seeking their own gratification. Utilitarian philosophy, which is connected with free-market economics, claimed that people always tried to gain pleasure and to avoid pain, so government should pass laws that promote the "greatest good of the greatest number" by maximizing the total amount of pleasure and minimizing the total amount of pain in society as a whole. Thus, Hobbes' basic approach remained influential through the nineteenth century.

# Hume's Emotivism

A second major school of empiricist ethics begins with David Hume's emotivism, which claimed that ethics is based on our moral sentiments.

Classical ethical theories said that we should subordinate our passions to our reason. Hume turned this idea upside-down by saying that, when it comes to determining how we should act, "reason is, and ought only to be, the slave of the passions, and can never pretend to any other office than to serve and obey them."[16] By this, he meant that reason cannot give us a motive for action. Our emotions give us a motive for acting by telling us what is good and bad, while our reason can only tell us the most effective means of getting what is good and avoiding what is bad.

Hume agreed with Hobbes' that ethics must be based on our feelings, but he disagreed with Hobbes' claim that we can base laws of behavior on observations of how people actually behave and what their actual appetites and aversions are, because Hume (as we have seen) believed that we cannot derive normative conclusions from factual observations.

Hume tried to avoid this error by basing his ethics on descriptions of how people use moral language, descriptions of what people mean when they say certain behavior is good and other behavior is bad. Examining our language, Hume found that our moral judgments are not based on feelings of self-interest, as Hobbes had claimed, but on feelings of benevolence toward others.

Hume gave many examples to show that, when people use moral language, they are describing judgments based on feelings of benevolence. For example, he said that we admire virtues even when they are so remote from us in time that they cannot benefit us, so we must be admiring the benefits they brought to other people. And he gave examples to show that, where there is a conflict between feelings of self-interest and feelings of benevolence, our moral judgment is based on what would be best for everyone, not just what would be best for ourselves.

Hume begins his *Enquiry Concerning the Principles of Morals* by saying that his goal is to examine moral language to see what feelings underlie it, and he concludes:

> Avarice, ambition, vanity, and all passions ... comprised under the denomination of self-love are here excluded from our theory concerning the origin of morals, not because they are too weak, but because they have not a proper direction for that purpose. The notion of morals, implies some sentiment common to all mankind, which recommends the same object to general approbation, and makes every man, or most men, agree in the same opinion or decision concerning it. ... When a man denominates another his *enemy*, his *rival*, his *antagonist*, his *adversary*, he is understood to speak the language of self-love, and to express sentiments, peculiar to himself and arising from his particular circumstances. But when he bestows on another man the epithets of *vicious* or *odious* or *depraved*, he then speaks another language, and expresses sentiments, in which, he expects, all his audience are to concur with him. He must here, therefore, depart from his private and particular situation, and must chuse a point of view, common to him with others ... If he means, therefore, to express, that this man possesses qualities whose tendency is pernicious to society, he has chosen this common point of view ....[17]

But this leaves Hume with a problem that he considers briefly at the end of his book on ethics. He has shown that people have complex motives, including feelings of self-love and feelings of benevolence, and that moral language is based on the feelings of benevolence. In the final section of his book, only four pages long, he asks why people *ought to* follow the moral principles based on their feelings of benevolence rather than following their feelings of self-interest, and he admits that he does not have a good answer:

> ...though it is allowed that, without a regard to property, no society could subsist; yet, according to the imperfect way which human affairs are conducted, a sensible knave, in particular incidents, may think that an act of iniquity or infidelity will make a considerable addition to his fortune, without causing any considerable breach in

the social union and confederacy. ... I must confess that, if a man think, that this reasoning much requires an answer, it will be a little difficult to find any, which will appear to him satisfactory. If his heart rebel not against such pernicious maxims, if he feel no reluctance to the thoughts of villainy or baseness, he has indeed lost a considerable motive to virtue ...[18]

Here, Hume admits that he cannot come up with a reason to follow one set of emotions rather than another. If you are the sort of person who follows your feelings of self-interest, there is nothing he can say to convince you that it is better to follow your feelings of benevolence – but he also is very confident that normal, decent people will not need any reasons and will simply see that they should act on their moral feelings.

Hume cannot give a reason for following your moral emotions rather than your self-interested emotions, because he believes that you cannot derive "ought statements" from "is statements." As an empiricist, he can show that people actually do make moral statements that are based on feelings of benevolence. But he cannot show you why you ought to act on these moral statements rather than on your self-interest.

## Empiricism Leads To Relativism

In both Hobbes' and Hume's versions of empiricism, reason cannot tell us what is good or bad. Judgments about good and bad are based on our feelings, and reason can only tell us the best way to gratify our feelings.

Unfortunately for ethical empiricism, Hobbes and Hume had totally different ideas about what sort of feelings are the basis of our moral judgments. Hobbes and the utilitarian philosophers who followed him claimed that ethics is based on feelings of self-interest. Hume and the line of philosophers who followed him believed that ethics is based on feelings of benevolence and sympathy for others.

But despite the different motives, Hobbes and Hume both believed in similar virtues and vices and both had similar views of the good life. Hobbes says people want the good life for themselves, and Hume says that they want it for society as a whole, but both Hobbes and Hume believe the good life consists of economic prosperity, pleasure, and respectability. They are very much British men of their time.

This sort of empiricist ethics seemed tenable in a society like the Britain of that time, where people generally had the same the same idea of the good life and were parochial enough to believe that people in all places and at all times felt very much as they did.

Hobbes believed that people in the primitive state of nature, before the social contract, were motivated by their own self-interest in competition with everyone else's self-interest, like the English capitalists of his own time. Likewise, Hume wrote:

> It is universally acknowledged that there is a great uniformity among the actions of men, in all nations and ages, and that human nature remains still the same in its principles and operations.[19]

It makes sense to build an ethical theory by examining the feelings that underlie people's moral judgments, only if you believe that all people have similar moral judgments. This empiricist ethics makes no sense if different groups of people have completely different moral judgments: empiricism cannot give us any reason to think that one moral system is better than another.

During the twentieth century, empiricism could not hold up against anthropologists who described primitive societies that had totally different moral systems than ours. For example, the anthropologist Ruth Benedict argued for moral relativism by describing the Zuni, whose lives center around performing of rituals, the Dobu, whose lives center around betraying others and protecting themselves from treachery, and the Kwakiutl, whose lives center around asserting their status by destroying and giving away their property.[20] This anthropological finding that there are people with totally different ideas of the good life than ours does not threaten other ethical theories, but it is disastrous for any empiricist ethics based on common feelings that underlie the common moral judgments of all people.

Likewise, empiricism could not withstand the attacks of modern philosophers who advanced a totally different idea of the good life from the conventional one. For example, when Nietzsche said that our strongest feeling is the will to power, and when he admired the moral system of primitive aristocratic societies where the goal of life is to dominate others and to be honored, he was deliberately attacking philosophers (like Hobbes and Hume) who based their moral theories on what they believed was the universal desire for prosperity, respectability and pleasure: "Man does not strive for pleasure," he wrote contemptuously, "only the Englishman does."[21]

Nietzsche talked about a "transvaluation of all values" that would overthrow the old slave values of classical philosophy and of Christianity. Nietzscheans were the first to describe the ethics of a society as its "values," a word that implies that there can be any number of completely different value systems. This new use of the word "values" spread among the general public during the twentieth century, as Victorian morality was unsettled and people realized that there were many different value systems that could replace it.

When there are many value systems in competition, empiricism cannot give us any reason for thinking that one is better than another.

## Logical Positivists and Ordinary Language Theorists

During the early twentieth century, the most important ethical empiricists were the logical positivists. Instead of looking for the common feelings that underlie all human moral judgments, they dismissed moral judgments by saying that they were nothing more than expressions of feeling. They called them "value judgments" rather than moral judgments, using Nietzsche's word that implies there are many possible value systems.

The logical positivists thought that "value judgments" are based on personal feelings. For example, A. J. Ayer said that someone who makes a value judgment expresses his feeling of approval or disapproval by saying something is "good" or "bad," and this is no different from someone who hits his finger with a hammer and expresses his feeling of pain by saying "ow."[22] Notice that the person who hits his finger does not *describe* his feeling by saying "I am in pain"; instead, he *expresses* his feeling by saying "ow." Likewise, the person who makes a value judgment does not describe his feeling by saying "I like this" or "I dislike this"; instead, he expresses his feeling by saying "this is good" or "this is bad."

This view is sometimes called the "Hurrah-Boo theory" of ethics, because it says that value judgments express people's feelings in just the same way as the cheers and boos of the spectators at a sporting event.

Critics of the positivists showed that the "Hurrah-Boo" theory was wrong because people do not disagree with statements about their feelings, but they do disagree about moral judgments. For example, if I say "ow" after hitting my finger with a hammer, no one would disagree with me, but if I say "What that man did was wrong," someone may disagree by saying "No, what he did was right."

Ordinary language theorists, such as R. M. Hare, built on this point and showed that moral judgments are meant to be universal. If you cheer for your team at a sporting event, you are not making any sort of general statement, but when you make a moral judgment, you imply that everyone who is in the same situation should act in the same way. For example, if you say that it is morally wrong for John Smith to abuse his children, you also imply that it is wrong for anyone to abuse his children.[23] The ordinary language theorists examined the ways in people use moral language at great length, but they did not give us any advice about what is a good life.

## The Failure of Empiricism

Hume described the language people use to make moral statements because he wanted to discover the shared moral sentiments underlying our moral judgments. After a long series of refinements by logical positivists and ordinary language theorists, we have learned something about the language that people use to make moral statements, but we have abandoned the original goal of basing ethics on the shared moral sentiments of humanity.

Early empiricists assumed that there was a common moral sense of humanity and that philosophers could identify the sentiments underlying it. But during the twentieth century, when they were faced with radically different moral systems, empiricists could not give us any reason for adopting one of these systems rather than another. They shifted to minute technical analysis of moral language because they could no longer deal with substantive questions about what is right or wrong.

Empiricism bases ethics on our feelings, but many different types of human feeling exist, and the empiricists have no reason for saying that some feelings are better than others. They cannot move from "is statements," telling us what feelings people actually have and what moral judgments people actually make, to "ought statements," telling us what moral judgments we should make.[24]

# Chapter 5

# Modernist Ethics: Rationalism

The rationalists were the other line of modern philosophers who tried to develop an ethical theory that did not depend on a teleological view of nature. These philosophers accepted the logical principle that you cannot derive "ought statements" from "is statements," but they reacted to this principle in the opposite way than the empiricists did.

The empiricists, as we saw in the previous chapter, describe how people actually use moral language. They describe what is, and they cannot reach valid conclusions about what ought to be.

The rationalists, whom we will look at in this chapter, try to develop ethical theories based on reason, and not on any facts about human nature. They try to reach conclusions about what ought to be without reference to what is.

## Kant's Practical Reason

During his early life, Immanuel Kant was a conventional philosopher of his time, but when he was in his late forties, he read the writings of David Hume, who (he said) "interrupted my dogmatic slumber."[25] After a decade of silence, he began when he was in his late fifties to produce books that changed the history of philosophy.

Kant was convinced by Hume that we cannot derive values from facts, but rather than developing a descriptive ethics like Hume's, Kant tried to develop an ethical theory based entirely on reason. His ideal was a theory that had nothing to do with the facts about human nature and that would apply equally to any rational being.

According to Kant, there is a faculty of practical reason that tells us what is right and wrong, which is different from the faculty pure reason that tells us what is true and false. Through our practical reason, we know the categorical imperative, which is the basis of all moral reasoning. One way of stating the categorical imperative is that we should always treat people as ends in themselves, not only as means to our ends. Another way of stating the same idea is that we should always act so we can will that the maxim governing our particular action should be a universal law governing everyone's behavior.

Kant said that we can derive two types of duties from the categorical imperative. There are perfect duties, which are necessary to avoid maxims that would be self-contradictory if they were universalized. And there are imperfect duties, which avoid maxims that would not quite be self-contradictory if they were universalized but which we cannot will because we would not want to live in a world where these maxims are universalized.

There is a perfect duty toward oneself: not to commit suicide. If someone commits suicide, he is acting out of self-love, and his maxim is that it is right to shorten one's own life to avoid pain or unhappiness. But this maxim cannot become a universal law of nature, according to Kant, because the function of self-love is to further life, and if it became a motive to destroy life, nature could not subsist. Killing yourself out of self-love "cannot possibly hold as a universal law of nature, and is therefore entirely opposed to the supreme principle of all duty."[26]

There is a perfect duty toward others: not to lie. We cannot will lying to be a universal law, because if everyone lied, it would be impossible to lie successfully: no one would believe that anything you said was true. When you try to make lying into a universal law, you can see that it is self-contradictory.

The prohibition against suicide and lying are the perfect duties toward yourself and others, because willing suicide and lying to become universal would be self-contradictory.

In addition, Kant said that there are two imperfect duties, one toward yourself and one toward others: you should develop your own talents, and you should help others. These are imperfect duties, because we can conceive of a world where people do not follow these laws. They are not like lying or suicide, which are self-contradictory and logically incoherent if we try to universalize them. However, we can see that a world where everyone followed these imperfect duties would be better than a world where people did not develop their own talents and did not help others.

The problem with Kant's theory is that the categorical imperative alone is not enough to give much content to ethics. It is plausible to say that the perfect duties are based purely on the categorical imperative (though the argument against suicide is far-fetched, because it is hard to believe that the entire system of nature would collapse if we adopted the universal law that people in extreme pain should kill themselves). But just saying that we should not commit suicide and should not lie is not enough to give any real content or direction to our lives.

And the imperfect duties, which could give direction to our lives, are not based purely on the categorical imperative, as Kant claims they are. They are actually based on observing human nature.

Kant says that we have an imperfect duty to develop our own talents, but he believes this only because he has observed human nature and seen that people have talents or potentials that they must work to develop. This duty would not apply to a rational being whose talents develop spontaneously, without any effort or work. This duty is similar to the principle of natural ethics that the virtues help us to develop our natural capabilities, and it is based on observation of human nature.

Kant also says we have an imperfect duty to help others, but what we mean by helping others depends on what we believe human nature is. We obviously should help others who are hungry by giving them food, but this is obvious because we can see clearly that human nature requires food. When we move beyond the necessities of human nature, it is not at all obvious what it means to help others. Does it mean to help them develop their capabilities, to help them maximize the amount of pleasure in their lives, to help them achieve salvation by accepting Christ as their savior, or to help them to achieve union with Brahman through meditation? What you think you should do to help others depends on what you think the good life is – and saying that we should help others does not tell you what the good life is.

Though Kant does not recognize it, you would have different imperfect duties to yourself and to others, depending on your view of human nature and of the good human life. If you believe the goal of life is to actualize your capabilities, you would want to develop your talents and help others to develop their talents. If you are a hedonist and believe the goal of life is to maximize pleasure, you would want to give yourself and others pleasure. If you are the Grand Inquisitor and you believe the goal of life is to go to heaven by practicing Catholic rituals, you would want to go to church regularly and to force others go to church regularly. If you are Timothy Leary and believe that the goal of life is to raise your consciousness by taking drugs, you would want to take as much LSD as possible and to give everyone else as much LSD as possible. In each case, you would prefer to live in a world where the maxims that govern your own behavior are universalized

To go beyond very narrow issues, such as the duty not to commit suicide and not to lie, to create an ethical theory with enough content to give real direction to our lives, you have to move beyond rationalism and look at human nature. If they had more content, Kant's imperfect duties to develop your own talents and to help other people could be very similar to the natural ethics sketched in Chapter 2 of this book. But Kant cannot give them much real content, because he cannot admit that they are based on observation of human nature, because he does not believe that you can derive normative statements from factual statements.

# Moore's Intuitionism

Intuitionism was the other important rationalist attempt to develop ethics based purely on reason, without deriving values from facts.

Intuitionists claim that our reason knows directly that certain things are good, in the same way that our reason knows directly that the axioms of geometry are true. The fact that these things are good does not need any further proof, any more than the axioms of geometry need further proof. (These philosophers use the word "intuition" to mean direct, certain, rational knowledge, such as the knowledge we have of the axioms of geometry. The word does not mean a guess or hunch, as it does in common speech.)

A number of minor philosophers took this position during the nineteenth century, reacting against Hume.

G. E. Moore, in the early twentieth century, was the most important philosopher who had this view. He agreed with the empiricists that you cannot derive "ought statements" from "is statements," but rather than the descriptive ethics of the empiricists (is without ought), he tried to develop purely rational ethics (ought without is).

Moore claimed that we have direct, rational knowledge that certain things are human goods, such as esthetic experience and friendship. Behavior is good if it helps bring us these human goods.

The problem with intuitionism is that it does not say anything about how these self-evident goods are related to each other or about why they are good. Each good is known through a separate, isolated intuition.

Because it lacks a theory that makes all the intuitions cohere, intuitionism does not let us move beyond the prejudices of our own time: there is no way of knowing whether you have a subjective feeling of certainty that something is a good because of real insight or because of ingrained prejudice. And because it lacks a larger theory, intuitionism does not give you any way of arguing against someone who does not have the same direct rational insights that you do.

George Moore himself believed that friendship and esthetic experience are the two most important self-evident goods because this was the conventional idea of the good life among his friends in Bloomsbury, but he had no way to move beyond these local prejudices and fit these two goods into a longer list of human goods. And he had no answers to people whose principles were different from his own, as we can see in Keynes' description of how Moore responded to people who disagreed with him:

How did we know what states of mind were good? This was a matter of ... direct unanalyzable intuition about which it was useless and impossible to argue. In that case, who was right when there was a difference of opinion? ... In practice, victory was with those who could speak with the greatest appearance of clear, undoubting conviction and could best use the accents of infallibility. Moore at this time was a master of this method – greeting one's remarks with a gasp of incredulity – *Do* you *really* think *that* ... as if to hear such a thing reduced him to a state of wonder verging on imbecility, with his mouth wide open and wagging his head in the negative so violently that his hair shook. *Oh!* he would say, goggling at you as if either you or he must be mad; and no reply was possible.[27]

Needless to say, if all philosophers used Moore's method of arguing, the discussion of ethics would not get very far.

Moore's ethical theory is like a theory of geometry that says that certain theorems (such as the theorem that the angles of a triangle add up to 180 degrees) are self-evidently true, but does not go any further by proving these theorems from axioms and postulates. This statement about triangles is correct, but we need to go further and derive all our theorems from a few underlying principles, so we can have a rational discussion with someone who does not see that the angles of a triangle add up to 180 degrees, rather than just making a face to show how shocked we are. And once we derive the theorems we know intuitively from a few underlying principles, we will also be able to generate more theorems than the ones we knew intuitively.

Likewise, Moore would have had a more coherent and complete theory if he had gone beyond listing the things that he knew intuitively were good and developed a general theory about why they were good. His self-evident goods fit perfectly well into our theory of natural ethics: they are good because they actualize natural capabilities. If Moore had gone beyond isolated intuitions to the general theory that goods actualize natural capabilities, he would have been able to argue against people who disagreed with him, rather than just making faces, and he would have been able to expand his list of goods to cover the entire range of human capabilities, rather than limiting himself to the favorite capabilities of his Bloomsbury set.

But he could not develop this broader theory, because he believed that you cannot derive values from facts about human nature.

# Catholic Modernists

The most important recent intuitionists are Catholic philosophers who have reinterpreted Thomas Aquinas' natural law theory so it does not violate the logical principle that that we cannot derive values from facts. The Catholic philosophers Germain Grisez, John Finnis and Joseph Boyle claim that we have a direct, rational knowledge that certain things are human goods, which is not based on observing human nature. In their view, natural law promotes human flourishing by letting people attain these intuitively self-evident goods.

Grisez, Finnis and Boyle claim that this is what Thomas Aquinas said all along, and that later Thomists misinterpreted him when they said he believed the moral law is based on human nature. They claim that Aquinas actually believed there is a separate faculty of practical reason that lets us know by intuition what are human goods.

It would be odd if Thomas Aquinas had really made exactly the same points that Kant and Moore made to get around the logical principle that we cannot derive values from facts – Kant's point that we have a separate faculty of practical reason that sees moral truths and Moore's point that we have a direct intuitive knowledge of the human good that is independent of our observation of human nature – considering that this logical principle was invented five hundred years after Thomas Aquinas lived. Actually, in the passages that these Catholic modernists point to, Aquinas just mentions practical reason in passing: he probably was talking about a practical use of the general faculty of reason, not about a separate faculty, though he says so little about it that it is hard to tell what he means.

Grisez, Finnis and Boyle have each come up with a list of the human goods that we know intuitively by reason – and their lists are slightly different. They cannot make their lists more consistent by admitting that all the items on the lists actualize potentials of human nature, because they accept the modernist idea you cannot derive values from facts about human nature.

# Chapter 6

# Facts and Values

Modern ethical theory has been stymied by the principle that ethics cannot be based on observation of human nature because it is logically impossible to derive normative conclusions from factual premises. In this view, "ought statements" and "is statements" are two logically different types of statements about the world, so you cannot derive one from the other. As we have seen, Hume was the first to make this claim, saying:

> … of a sudden I am surpris'd to find that instead of the usual copulation of propositions, is, and is not, I meet with no proposition that is not connected with an ought or an ought not. This change is imperceptible; but is, however, of the last consequence. For as this *ought*, or *ought not*, expresses some new relation or affirmation, it is necessary that it should be observed and explained; and at the same time that a reason should be given, for what seems altogether unconceivable, how this new relation can be a deduction from others, which are entirely different from it.[28]

We obviously cannot come to conclusions about what is based on premises about what ought to be. Hume and the ethicists who followed him believed that we just as obviously cannot come to conclusions about what ought to be based on premises about what is, because these are two different types of relation or affirmation.

We have seen that, because of this principle, modern ethical theory has been empiricist, talking about the "is" without the "ought," or rationalist, talking about the "ought" without the "is."

But despite its great historical influence, the idea that it is logically impossible to derive "ought statements" from "is statements" is simply an error.

In this chapter, we will look at some cases where you have two "is statements" as premises and you very obviously can derive an "ought statement" (but not an "is statement") from them as a conclusion.

We will see that it is logically possible to derive "ought statements" from teleological "is statements" – statements about function, purpose, intention or some other telos.

We will distinguish between "ought statements" that aim at some arbitrarily chosen end and "ought statements" that aim at some natural end. We will call these two types of statements conditional imperatives and natural imperatives.

# Conditional Imperatives

A conditional imperative (or "hypothetical imperative," as Kant would have called it) tells us that we ought to do something in order to achieve some end we have chosen but not that we have an absolute moral obligation to do it.

For example, if someone stops me on the street and says he is lost and wants to go to the library, I might answer him by saying, "You ought to walk three blocks straight ahead."

But I am not using the word "ought" in an absolute moral sense here: if the person is going to the library to steal books or to murder the librarian, then (in the absolute moral sense) he should not go there at all. My statement really means, "In order to get to the library, you ought to walk three blocks straight ahead."

We can formulate my advice to this person as a syllogism with two premises that are "is statements" and a conclusion that is an "ought statement":

Your goal is to walk to the library.
The library is three blocks straight ahead.
In order to walk to the library, you ought to walk three blocks straight ahead.

Notice that is not possible to draw a *factual* conclusion from these two factual premises. You cannot conclude "In order to walk to the library, you *will* walk three blocks straight ahead," because something may prevent you from actually walking there. From these two factual premises, the only conclusion you can derive is the "ought statement": "In order to walk to the library, you *ought to* walk three blocks straight ahead."

This example shows very clearly that Hume and the ethicists who followed him were wrong to say that "is statements" as premises can only lead to "is statements" as conclusions, not to "ought statements."

# Natural Imperatives

A natural imperative tells us that we should do something for the sake of a natural end. For example, we should exercise and avoid smoking so our lungs can carry oxygen to our bodies, or we should give food to people who are starving so they can live. In this case, we do not choose the purpose arbitrarily: it given by nature.

Here is a syllogism that lets us derive a natural imperative from two "is statements":

The function of the lungs is to supply the body with oxygen.
Exercise increases the ability of the lungs to supply the body with oxygen.
For your lungs to supply your body with oxygen well, you ought to exercise.

Likewise, this syllogism lets us derive a negative natural imperative from two "is statements":

The function of the lungs is to supply the body with oxygen.
Smoking cigarettes reduces or destroys the ability of the lungs to supply the body with oxygen.
For your lungs to supply your body with oxygen well, you ought not to smoke cigarettes.

These syllogisms are similar to the syllogism used above to derive a conditional imperative. Here, too, it is not possible to draw a factual conclusion from these factual premises, only an imperative conclusion. You cannot conclude that you *will* exercise and *will not* smoke, only that you *ought to* exercise and *ought not to* smoke.

If we expand these syllogisms by adding the premises "It is good for any natural capability to function well" and "We ought to pursue the good," we can drop the conditional clause from the conclusion and simply conclude: "You ought to exercise" and "You ought not to smoke cigarettes."

Because it is self-evident that it is good for any natural capability to function well and that we ought to pursue the good, we can state these natural imperatives without the conditional clause, just as the doctor does when he tells you, without any qualification, that you ought to exercise and that you ought not to smoke cigarettes.

These natural imperatives are the maxims of natural ethics that let humans and other living creatures flourish.

# Practical Syllogisms

The syllogisms we have just looked at are related to what logicians call practical syllogisms, syllogisms that have two factual premises and have an action as their conclusion. Though Aristotle did not use this term, historians of philosophy always trace practical syllogisms back to his discussion of syllogisms that lead to action.

Aristotle uses examples where the major premise is simply a desire: "I want to drink, says appetite; this is drink, says sense or imagination; and straightway I drink." He explains that "the actualization of desire is a substitute for inquiry or reflection."

Aristotle also uses examples where the major premise is a universal imperative based on understanding human nature: "one conceives that every man ought to walk, one is a man oneself: straightway one walks," explaining that "the mind does not stop to consider an obvious minor premise; for example, if walking is good for man, one does not dwell upon the minor 'I am a man.'"[29]

The first of these examples is related to what we call conditional imperatives, and the second is related to what we call natural imperatives.

There is one difference between the conclusions of practical syllogisms and "ought statements." Practical syllogisms lead immediately to action. If some interruption prevents immediate action, then you make an "ought statement" instead of acting.

For example, if I want to go to the library and I know where it is, there is no interruption and I can simply act. We have the practical syllogism:

My goal is to walk to the library.
I know that the library is three blocks straight ahead.
*(There is no verbal conclusion. The conclusion is that I walk three blocks straight ahead.)*

43

However, when there are interruptions that prevent immediate action, similar syllogisms conclude with an "ought statement" rather than an action.

For example, there is an interruption if the person who acts does not know all of the factual premises. This is what happens when someone stops me on the street to ask for directions to the library, and I tell her to walk three blocks ahead. There is a interruption before the action, because she knows that she wants to go to the library, but she does not know where the library is. After she tells me that her goal is to go to the library, I know the two factual premises, so I can form the syllogism:

Your goal is to walk to the library *(which she told me).*
The library is three blocks straight ahead *(which I already know).*
In order to walk to the library, you ought to walk three blocks straight ahead *(which I tell her, because I know the two factual premises and can draw this conclusion).*

If she knew both of the factual premises herself, there would be a practical syllogism instead of an ought statement: she would simply walk to the library rather than stating a verbal conclusion. Since I know both premises but I am not the one who acts on them, the syllogism leads to an "ought statement" rather than an immediate action. I make the verbal "ought statement" that tells her to take the action.

The conclusion could also be an ought statement rather than an action, if I am acting on a practical syllogism but I am threatened by some sort of interruption. For example, I begin with the same practical syllogism as before:

My goal is to walk to the library.
I know that the library is three blocks straight ahead.
*(There is no verbal conclusion. The conclusion is that I begin walking to the library.)*

But on the way to the library, I pass a bakery, and I am tempted to stop and eat, even though stopping will not leave me with enough time to do my work in the library. At this point, rather than just continuing to walk straight ahead without thinking, I might stop to look in the bakery window and then say to myself:

I ought to walk straight ahead.

Here, I am verbally stating the conclusion to what was a practical syllogism in order to encourage myself to keep walking rather than being stopped by this interruption.

Moralistic "ought statements" generally work this way. There is something that I know I ought to do, but I have some desire that conflicts with my doing it, so I make an "ought statement" to encourage myself to do what I should. When I feel like eating too much, I remind myself that "I ought to keep my weight down," when I feel lazy, I remind myself that "I ought to go to the gym and exercise," and when I feel like lying to someone to swindle him out of his money, I remind myself that "I ought to be honest."

No doubt, we could give other examples of when people use practical syllogisms that lead to action, and when they use normative syllogisms that lead to "ought statements." But here, we just need to point out that, if two factual premises can imply an action as their conclusion, as Aristotle says of practical syllogisms, then two factual premises can also imply an "ought statement" as their conclusion, because an "ought statement" is simply a recommended action.

# Human Nature and the Good

Most philosophers since Hume and Kant have said that we can not derive moral principles from observations of human nature, because they believed it was logically impossible to derive "ought statements" from "is statements."

In reality, we can use the sort of natural imperative described above to derive "ought statements" from observations of human nature that tell us about the inherent goals or functions of people's natural capabilities. Once we see that there is a natural capability with an inherent telos, we can conclude that we ought to do what is needed to allow the capability to achieve its telos.

There are some capabilities that everyone would agree on. Everyone can see that our lungs have the function of breathing, and therefore we ought to exercise because it helps the lungs function well, and we ought not to smoke cigarettes because it prevents the lungs from functioning well.

Likewise, everyone can see that there is a human ability to understand things, so it is good to be intelligent and bad to be stupid, and that there is a human ability to make music, so it is good to be musically talented and bad to be tone deaf. In each of these cases, we ought to do things that develop these abilities, such as studying to develop our intelligence, and we ought not to do things that destroy these abilities, such as drinking so much that we destroy brain cells and dull our intelligence.

In addition to these obvious capabilities, though, there have been human capabilities that people have disagreed about.

There are obvious historic examples of cases where cultures have discovered capabilities that earlier cultures did not know about. Presumably, even the earliest humans realized that it is good to be healthy and bad to be sick, good to be strong and bad to be weak. Yet primitive societies did not know that people are capable of reading and writing. After literacy was invented and societies realized reading and writing are important human capabilities, they virtually all agreed that it is good to be literate and bad to be illiterate. Today, we agree there is something wrong with someone who has a disability that prevents them from ever learning to read, and there is something wrong when someone is denied an education and does not have the opportunity to learn to read.[30] Once we understand the factual premise that people have the capability of reading, we accept these normative conclusions.

Historically, disputes about the rights of different groups of people often depended on claims about their natural capabilities. For example, men argued that, because women were emotional rather than rational, they did not have the capability to become fully educated or to manage their own business affairs. When women began to do these things, they showed that they did have these capabilities, which was used as evidence that they ought to be educated and independent so these capabilities could be fully developed. The factual premise that they had these capabilities led to the normative conclusion that they ought to be allowed to develop these capabilities.

Again, in most cultures at most times, people believed that it was good to follow society's customs and rituals without questioning them. Philosophers in classical Greece, and most people in the West after the Protestant Reformation and the Enlightenment, began to believe that we have the capability of using our conscience and our reason to decide what is right and wrong; therefore they believed that people should have freedom of conscience and freedom of thought to let them develop this capability. This capability still is not universally acknowledged: there are still religious authorities who claim that ordinary people should follow their doctrines unquestioningly, because people are not capable of deciding these questions for themselves.

These historical examples show that disagreements about human nature – factual disagreements about what capabilities people have – lead to disagreements about how people ought to live. The different factual premises lead to different normative conclusions.

There is no logical problem that stands in the way of deriving values from the facts about human nature. A teleological "is statement" can imply an "ought statement," and statements about human capabilities can imply "ought statements' because they involve implicit teleology.

When medical studies first showed that smoking reduces lung capacity and can cause lung cancer and emphysema, everyone saw that these "is statements" implied that people "ought to" give up smoking – and even philosophers should be able to accept this obvious conclusion.

# Chapter 7

# The Sciences Versus Scientism

Classical natural ethics was not abandoned because it is logically impossible to derive "ought statements" from "is statements." It was abandoned because the west moved from a teleological view to a non-teleological view of nature.

When Hume first suggested that you cannot derive normative statements from factual statements, he was reacting against philosophers like Hobbes, who tried to base ethics on the new physics. Hobbes claimed that matter moves in the ways that the physicists describe, mechanically causing our appetites and aversions, and that therefore we ought to base ethics on these appetites and aversions. Hume was right to say that you cannot derive "ought statements" from this sort of non-teleological "is statement." There is no more reason to base ethics on these mechanical causes than there is to base ethics on the fact that gravity makes rocks fall downward.

If you have a non-teleological view of nature as a whole, then it is plausible to claim that you cannot derive normative statements from factual statements about nature, and philosophers like Hume and Kant had this view of nature in the back of their minds when they rejected the attempt to base ethics on human nature.

Today's philosophers sometimes say that we cannot revive natural ethics because we cannot go back to a teleological view of nature, like Aristotle's. But in fact, the philosophers who tried to use the new physics to explain everything just replaced one dogmatic view of nature with another.

The Aristotelians were dogmatic to explain all of nature in teleological terms – to explain even the movement of falling stones in terms of final causes. They took the bit that they did know about biology, and they used it to explain all of nature.

Materialist philosophers from Hobbes onward were just as dogmatic when they tried to explain all of nature in terms of the new physics – to explain even the behavior of animals and people solely in terms of mechanical causes. They took the bit that they did know about the motion of matter, and they used it to explain all of nature.

In fact, we do not have a single totalizing theory that lets understand nature as a whole. We can understand the motion of inanimate matter in terms of mechanical causes, but we cannot understand living organisms without also thinking about function: the function of a plant's leaves is to gather sunlight, the function of the eye is to see, the function of the intellect is to understand, and so on.

Modernist philosophers replaced the old dogmas of scholasticism with the new dogmas of scientism. Individual sciences let us understand parts of nature. Scientism uses the individual sciences as a starting point for purely speculative totalizing theories that explain everything.

In fact, we can see that inanimate matter moves according to the laws of physics, that life developed according to the laws of evolutionary biology, and that human reasoning is valid if it follows the laws of logic. But we have not found one set of scientific laws that explains it all, from the big bang, to the human intellect, to the validity of the laws of science that are discovered by the human intellect.

We can understand pieces of nature, but we do not have a single theory that explains everything, so there is no value to windy generalizations about everything, such as "we cannot go back to a teleological view of nature."

# We Do Not Know Everything

We do not know everything. It is important to emphasize this obvious point only because so much modernist philosophy has tried to take the findings of one science and turn them into an explanation of everything.

In the seventeenth and eighteenth centuries, the new physics was considered a totalizing science that could explain the entire world, because the world was made up of matter in motion. Descartes excepted human behavior from this total theory: he believed that the behavior of plants and animals could be explained purely in terms of mechanical causes but that the human soul and free will existed in addition to matter. In the eighteenth century, Descartes' follower La Mettrie claimed that there was no need to talk about the soul and free will: like animal behavior, human behavior could be explained purely in terms of mechanical causes.

By the nineteenth century, physical determinism was so influential that Laplace wrote in 1812 that, if we knew the location and current motion of every particle in the universe, we could predict the entire future as certainly as we now predict the future location of the planets, because human behavior was governed by the same laws of physics that govern the motion of the planets:

> If we imagine an intellect which at any given moment knew all the forces that animate Nature and the mutual positions of the beings that comprise it – if this intellect were vast enough to submit its data to analysis, could condense into a single formula the movement of the greatest bodies of the universe and that of the lightest atom: for such an intellect nothing could be uncertain and the future just like the past would be present before its eyes.[31]

In this view, the laws of Newtonian physics explain everything, and they could, in principle let us predict future human history as we predict the future locations of the planets.

# Multiple Sciences

As physical determinism became more influential, however, the nineteenth century developed the new sciences of economics and evolutionary biology, which began to rival the claims of physics to be the totalizing science that could explain everything.

Marxists claimed that the laws of economics were the key: we could understand a society's ideas about politics, about ethics, and even about the physical sciences as an intellectual superstructure that was based on that society's economic substructure. Marx himself was unclear about the status of the physical sciences, but by the beginning of the twentieth century, there were Marxist pragmatists who argued that there were no objective sciences, that even sciences such as physics could all be explained as the result of economic interest and could be true only in the sense that they were historically successful.

Evolutionists claimed that theories of Darwin were the key to understanding everything. Herbert Spencer said that the development of the stars from diffused gas, the development of animal species, and the development of human societies, could all be explained by using the same basic law – the natural tendency to evolve from simpler, less differentiated forms to more complex and differentiated forms. Undifferentiated clouds of gas evolved into systems of stars and planets. One-celled organisms evolved into animals with specialized organs. Primitive societies where people all performed the same economic roles evolved into modern societies where people perform specialized economic roles. During the twentieth century, Darwinian pragmatists argued that human intellect is another trait that people evolved in order to survive, so it does not give us any objective knowledge: even sciences such as physics can only be true in the sense that they are useful for the success of the species.

There have been at least three sciences which philosophers claimed were the one key to understanding the universe: physics, economics, and evolutionary biology. But these three sciences have different laws, and the laws of one cannot be reduced to the laws of another. It should be clear that each of these sciences is based on a different body of observations – which means that each theory explains only some of our observations, and none explains everything.

Physics is based on observations of inanimate matter in motion. But the laws of motion tell us nothing about which species are fit to survive: if we knew the location and motion of all matter, as Laplace imagined, it might conceivably let us predict when life would first appear on earth because of chemical combinations of matter, but it clearly would not let us predict which species would be fit to survive and which would not.

Once the laws of physics led matter to form molecules that can replicate themselves, then a new law of evolutionary biology emerged: traits will become more common if they make these molecules and their descendents more fit to survive and to reproduce themselves. This law of survival of the fittest cannot be reduced to the laws of Newtonian physics.

Likewise, once life has evolved to the point where it produces people who calculate their own self-interest and who have a money economy, you can describe their behavior based on the principles of economics. If we knew the location and motion of all matter, it would not let us predict which means of production would win out against others in the market. The laws of economics cannot be reduced to the laws of Newtonian physics or to the laws of evolution.

Today, individual sciences are discovering their own limits. Chaos theory has shown that we cannot predict precisely the behavior of complex systems, and quantum mechanics has shown that there is a random element to physics. These developments in physics have exploded Laplace's idea that the laws of physics could let us predict the future, even the future of systems made up purely of matter in motion. This is the conventional view of why Laplace was wrong.

But here, we are looking at a broader epistemological limit on any science. When we look at all the different sciences that exist today, it should be clear that each science chooses a body of observations that it can make sense of. Physics, evolutionary biology, and economics have become sciences because each has a theory that explains the observations it deals with, but they can do this only because each focuses on its own subject, on the one piece of the universe that it can explain, and ignores many other things that we observe. For example, physicists look at the behavior of inanimate matter, not at animal behavior or human behavior.

Today, physicists are working on what they sometimes call a "theory of everything" that would unify relativity and quantum theory, but despite the name, no one believes that this theory could let us predict future human behavior or predict future political developments. It is hard for us to imagine that, in Laplace's day, many philosophers and scientists thought that Newtonian physics could, in principle, let us do just that: they thought that predicting future human history is the same sort of problem in physics as predicting future eclipses of the moon, except that it requires more data and more complex equations.

Today, we should be able to see that none of the sciences can explain everything. Each has picked out a mind-sized chunk of our experience to explain. Each has picked out its chunk precisely because it is a chunk that we are capable of understanding.

# The Ideal of Progress

As there were attempts to base ethics on physics during the seventeenth and eighteenth centuries (such as Hobbes'), there have been attempts to base ethics on evolutionary biology and on economics during the nineteenth and twentieth century. Evolution and economics were congenial to philosophers of the time, because they fit in with that era's widespread belief in progress: you could use either evolution or economics to discern a pattern in the past, and then you project this pattern into the future to determine the direction of progress.

But once we recognize that "ought statements" can only be derived from teleological "is statements," we can easily see the flaws in these attempts to base our idea of the good life on evolutionary progress or on economic progress, or on any other non-teleological description of the actual course of events.

Evolutionism, running from Herbert Spencer to some recent New Age thinkers, assumes that the process of evolution can be the basis of ethics. Since life evolved from with simple single-celled organisms to more complex organisms with specialized organs, since society evolved from simple tribal economies to complex modern economies with specialized work, it is good for society to keep evolving by becoming more complex and more specialized. As cities become bigger and more complex, as the world economy becomes more interdependent and complex, as the division of labor becomes more specialized and complex, our society becomes more advanced and more "evolved." The assumption is that evolution has taken us along this path in the past, and so it is good to continue on this path in the future.

Economism, in the style of Marx and other technological optimists, involves a similar faith in progress. In this view, history is the story of man's growing control over nature – from primitive people who are at the mercy of nature, to early civilizations that learned to farm and build irrigation projects, to industrial societies that learned to mine coal and build steam engines to harness energy that nature has stored, to the societies of the future that will use science to control all the forces of nature. Economic progress has increased our control of nature in the past, and so it good to continue increasing our control over nature in the future.

The believers in evolutionary progress and in economic progress all commit the fallacy of arguing from non-teleological "is-statements" to "ought-statements." They try to derive "ought statements" from "is statements" about what has actually happened in the past.

In reality, we can only derive these "ought" statements from teleological "is statements" that describe function or purpose. The function of impulses that evolved biologically is to help individuals to live and species to survive, and it is good for individuals to live and species to survive. The purpose of economic behavior is to provide people with necessities and comforts, and it is good to provide people with necessities and comforts. The function or purpose provides the standard that lets us decide which impulses and which economic institutions are good.

**Evolution and Ethics**

To give a simple example from evolutionary biology, humans evolved to like the taste of high-fat foods, because the food supply was not secure when the human species evolved: there was feast or famine, and people who ate fatty foods and gained weight when food was available were more likely to survive when food was scarce. Since we evolved this impulse, does it follow that it is good for people today to eat fatty foods and become overweight? Obviously not.

When we reason from evolution to ethics, we must look at the telos or function of the trait that evolved, not at the trait itself. The biological function of our impulse to eat fatty food was to help people to survive and remain healthy, and everyone agrees that it is good to survive and be healthy. Gaining weight served this biological function when our species was evolving because the food supply was insecure, but it no longer serves this function today, when we have a secure food supply and obesity has become a major health threat, a cause of diabetes, heart disease, and strokes.

When the food supply was insecure, eating high-fat food and gaining weight helped protect your health. Now that we have an abundant and secure food supply, eating low-fat food and avoiding being overweight is the way to protect your health, and everyone agrees that this is how we should eat. No one believes that people today ought to over-eat fatty foods because we have this impulse as the result of evolution. What we ought to do depends on the end for which the impulse evolved, protecting health, not on the actual impulse that evolved.

## Economics and Ethics

To give an example from economics, it was good for economies to became increasingly complex and to have increasing power over the forces of nature in the past, because that allowed economies to do the best job of providing necessities and comforts when there was an urgent need to increase production. It does not follow that we should keep moving to ever more complex economies with ever more control over the forces of nature in the future. To achieve the purpose of economic behavior in the future, we should move toward the economy that does the best job of providing people with necessities and comforts. What we ought to do is based on the end for which economies developed, not on the actual ways in which the economy developed.

There is an important difference between evolution and economic behavior: evolution is always based on natural ends, but economic behavior sometimes is not. Usually, the purpose of people's economic behavior is to provide themselves with food, clothing, shelter, education, and other goods that help them actualize their natural capabilities, but economic behavior can also be aimed at gaining money for its own sake. Traditionally, avarice was recognized as a vice because it is a form of unnatural economic behavior: misers accumulate money for its own sake, and they do not see that money is a means rather than an end, that money is useful only when it helps our natures to flourish. Today's cult of economic growth is also a form of unnatural economic behavior: we use advertising and government policy to convince people to buy more products purely to encourage economic growth, without asking whether these products help our natures to flourish or whether they just waste our time in getting and spending.

Our belief in economic progress, based on projecting the historical trend toward increased economic complexity and growth, now gets in the way of the real economic progress, progress toward living more satisfying lives.

# The Modernist Fallacy

The key error of scientism is that it begins with theories about the nature of the entire universe or of human knowledge, the theories we are least certain of, and it uses them to discredit ideas that we can be much more certain of.

This fallacy has been typical of many branches of philosophy since the seventeenth century. For example, in the case of epistemology, a modernist theory might begin by saying that all knowledge is based on sense experience, and it might use this idea as the basis of a theory that shows it is not really true that 2+2=4, because that statement just depends on our definition of words and tells us nothing about the world. Or in the case of ethics, a modernist theory might begin by saying that all that exists is matter, and it might use this idea as the basis of a theory that shows there is no objective ethics, so it is not really objectively wrong to murder an innocent person.

But we are more certain that 2+2=4 than we are that all knowledge is based on sense experience. And we are more certain that it is wrong to murder an innocent person than we are that nothing but matter exists. In cases like these, where they contradict one another, we should stick with the small ideas that we are more certain of, not with the theories of the entire universe and of all knowledge that we are less certain of.

Modernists accept empiricism or materialism – grand theories about things that we know very little about – because people today have the same irrational faith in "science" that people used to have in revealed religion. This is the modernist fallacy: modernists use the real discoveries of the sciences about their own subject matters as the basis of total explanations of the universe – and they have such faith that they believe these vague totalizing theories even when they contradict the bits of real knowledge that we do have.

Ordinary people do the same thing as philosophers. If you say that there can be objectively valid moral standards, people who have not studied philosophy and have just picked up conventional modern ideas will criticize you by saying: "Where do these standards come from? The universe is made of matter, and life evolved from matter by chance. How could this process possibly create any objectively valid moral values?" They do not see that we understand it is wrong to murder an innocent person much more clearly than we understand the entire universe.

## Existentialism Is A Modernism

Sartre's existentialism is a particularly blatant example of the modernist fallacy. Sartre argues that the objects we make have a purpose, so we can say that they are good if they fulfill this purpose: for example, the essential nature of a knife is to cut because it was made for that purpose, and so a knife is good if it cuts well. According to Sartre, people used to believe that we humans were made by God, so they believed that there is an essential human nature that determines what is good for us, based on God's purpose in creating us. But today, we modern people know that there is no God, so we know there is no essential human nature that determines what is good for us. Therefore, Sartre concludes, our existence precedes our essence: we have the freedom to make our own choices that define our own essence.[32]

Sartre is so dogmatic about the nature of the universe and God, which we do not really understand, that he denies the fact that there is a human nature, which we do clearly understand.

How can anyone take this idea of Sartre's seriously? If it were literally true that there is no human nature and we are free to define our own essence, then I could decide that I want to define myself as a wheezer, so that it is best for me to inhale smoke until I get emphysema, because that is my essence. I could define myself as a monopod, so it is best for me to cut off one of my legs and hop around on the one remaining leg, because that is my essence. I could define myself as a dog, so it is best for me to sniff people and bark at them instead of talking to them, because that is my essence. If we had the freedom to define our own essence, I could make the decision to define myself in any of these ways. These decisions would not be contrary to human nature, if there were no human nature.

In reality, we have freedom to act according to our nature or against our nature. We can decide not to smoke and protect our lungs, or we can decide to smoke and hurt our lungs. We can decide to study and improve our minds, or we can decide to watch trash television and let our minds stagnate. We also have freedom to decide which of our many natural capabilities we will focus on developing. But we do not have the freedom to redefine ourselves as wheezers, so it is good for us to smoke until we have emphysema because that is the essence of the wheezer. And we do not have the freedom to redefine ourselves as couch potatoes, so it is good for our minds to stagnate because that is the essence of the couch potato.

We know that it is good to be healthy and bad to be sick, and we know that it good to be knowledgeable and bad to be ignorant, with much more certainty than we know anything that Sartre says about God and the entire universe. Sartre is a perfect example of scientism, because he never showed interest in any particular science, only in vague, windy ideas about what science says is the nature of the universe.

## Classical Versus Traditional Values

It is important to emphasize that, by rejecting this sort of modernist ethics, we are not supporting the "traditional values" that conservatives call for. On the contrary, natural ethics was often used historically to argue for social change by showing that the status quo stultified human powers.

Socrates was executed for corrupting the youth and undermining traditional values. Philosophers in the main classical tradition of philosophical ethics – Aristotle and the peripatetics, the cynics and the stoics – believed ethics was based on human nature, and so they were willing (in the case of the cynics, were eager) to defy conventional values when they were contrary to nature.

Natural ethics was used by the abolitionist, feminist and civil rights movement to argue that slavery and discrimination stultified large groups of people by refusing to let them develop their natural powers.

These movements criticized the conventional values of their society in the name of human nature, while existentialists and other moral relativists criticize conventional values in the name of arbitrarily willed values.

# Chapter 8

# Ethics and Knowledge

Since the seventeenth century, modernists have believed that new scientific knowledge would sweep away earlier beliefs. The model was the new physics, which showed that many of the ideas of Aristotelian physics were false. For example, Aristotle believed that heavy bodies fell more quickly than light bodies and that the motion of inanimate matter had final causes. The new physics showed that these ideas are completely false.

Modernists believed that, just as the new physics swept away Aristotelian physics, science would sweep away metaphysics and superstition and let us understand the world once and for all. Hobbes led the way, by trying to develop a theory of ethics and politics based on the new physics to sweep away older natural law ethics.

But physics is not the only example of how knowledge changes and progresses. When we think about the history of many different bodies of knowledge, we get a different view of the progress of knowledge than these modernists had.

## The Progress of Knowledge

When we look at a number of different bodies of knowledge, we can see that the model of sweeping away the past does not always apply.

In some cases, new bodies of knowledge did sweep away old ideas. Newtonian physics showed that Aristotelian physics was false. Twentieth-century physics showed that Newton's basic assumptions about the nature of time, space, and matter were false. If physicists ever develop a theory that unifies relativity and quantum mechanics, it will presumably show that some basic ideas of twentieth-century physics were false.

In other cases, new bodies of knowledge developed where there were no older ideas at all. Before the science of ecology was developed, nobody thought about how communities of animals and plants depend on one another so changes in the population of one species affect other species.

Overall, it seems that there has been progress in knowledge, because more and more bodies of knowledge have been developed and established as reliable.

For example, plane geometry has been an established body of knowledge since the time of Euclid. Non-Euclidian geometries helped us to understand the nature and limits of Euclidian geometry, but they did not sweep it away; instead, they showed that it is one of many possible geometries. There is no possibility that a new geometry will show that triangles in a plane do not really obey the theorem of Pythagoras, as the new physics showed that matter does not really obey Aristotle's rule that heavy bodies fall faster than light bodies.

Arithmetic has been an established body of knowledge at least since the advent of decimal numerals. Number theory and other systems of notation (such as binary and hexadecimal numerals) have helped us to understand the nature of arithmetic and have given us new ways to do arithmetic, but they did not sweep away decimal arithmetic. There is no possibility that a new arithmetic will show that the multiplication table is wrong.

Chemistry has been an established body of knowledge since the periodic table of the elements was developed. Quantum mechanics helps us understand why elements have a certain maximum number of electrons in each ring, making them combine as they do, but there is no possibility that a new chemistry will show that elements combine in totally different ways than the periodic table predicts or that it will replace the elements in the periodic table with an entirely new set of elements, as the elements of earth, air, water, and fire were replaced by the periodic table.

Perhaps the theory of natural ethics is clear enough that it can also become an established body of knowledge, if we clean up some of the cobwebs that obscure it. We will not discover one day that it is good to be sick and bad to be healthy or that it is good to be ignorant and bad to be knowledgeable, any more than we will discover that the multiplication table and the periodic table are wrong.

Yet the basic principles of natural ethics, which we do understand, have always been muddied by theological questions and by epistemological questions – by theories about the nature of the entire universe and about the nature of our knowledge, which we do not understand. When Aristotle said that intellectual contemplation and moral virtue were our most important capabilities because we should do as much as we can to elevate ourselves to the level of the divine, when Sartre said that there is no God so there is no human nature, and when Hobbes said that the universe is made up of matter in motion so ethics must be based on feelings created by the motion of matter, they were all muddying or denying the clear principles of natural ethics for the sake of a much less clear theory about the total nature of the universe. When Hume said that ethics must be based on sentiment and when Kant said that ethics must be based on the faculty of practical reason, they were muddying or denying the clear principles of natural ethics for the sake of a much less clear theory about the basis of human knowledge.

Ethics can become clear only if we take a more modest approach that disentangles it from vague theories about the nature of the universe and of human knowledge, just as mathematics became a clear body of knowledge only after it was disentangled from the mysticism and idealism of Pythagoras and Plato. Philosophers are still arguing about whether mathematics gives us insight about a real world of pure ideas, as Plato said, but because we have disentangled mathematics from theology, these epistemological arguments do not prevent us from having confidence in geometry and arithmetic.

This more modest approach, which refuses to go beyond the ideas we can understand clearly, does limit the theory of ethics presented in this book. Because we do not claim to understand the purpose of life and the universe, we cannot arrange natural goods in a hierarchy on the basis of how important they are to the overall purpose of life, and we cannot see whether there is any transcendent theological good that is more important than these natural goods.

But this more modest approach does let us establish some fundamental points very clearly, because we do understand clearly the telos of each human capability. Because the function of the lungs is to deliver oxygen to the body, it is good to have high aerobic capacity and bad to have emphysema or asthma. Because one function of the intellect is to understand the world, it is good to be intelligent and knowledgeable and bad to be stupid and ignorant.

More generally, because health means that all our basic physical capabilities are functioning well, we can see clearly that health is good for people, animals and plants. And because arete means that all our human capabilities are functioning well, we can see clearly that arete is good for people.

This is not enough to explain the universe and the ultimate meaning of our lives, but it is enough to tell us that it is good to feed the hungry, to heal the sick, and to avoid the vices that damage our health and dull our abilities.

Any understanding we might have about the telos of human life as a whole is no more valid logically than our understanding that the telos of the lungs is to bring oxygen to our bodies, or our understanding of the telos of any other individual capability. The big issues are more important than the smaller issues, but they are much less certain than the smaller issues. Our understanding of the big issues is not logically prior to our understanding of the smaller issues, so we should begin with the small issues we can understand, rather than muddying them by beginning with the big issues we do not understand.

# Natural Ethics

After we separate the narrow subject of ethics from the big, vague questions about the nature of the universe and the ultimate meaning of life, we find that what we know about natural ethics is similar to what we know about health and illness.

Everyone can understand that health is the proper functioning of the body's organs, and that this involves a sort of natural teleology. The function of the eyes is to see, the function of the lungs is to bring the body oxygen, the function of the legs is to move you around. You are healthy if the organs perform these function well, and you are ill or disabled if the organs do not perform these functions well.

Everyone agrees that we should behave in ways that help our organs to function well. You should behave in ways that help protect your own health: for example, you should exercise and you should not smoke to protect your lungs and heart. And you should behave in ways that help protect other people's health: for example, you should cover your mouth when you sneeze to avoid spreading infection, and you should not dump toxic wastes in the river and poison people downstream.

No one says that we can no longer believe that health is good and illness is bad because modern science shows that "we cannot go back to a teleological view of nature." On the contrary, science has let us understand the telos of the organs more clearly than we used to. For example, people always knew that the function of the eye is to see. Now we also know that the function of the lens of the eye is to focus light on the retina. If the lens is not performing this function properly, we correct it with glasses or with laser surgery, so the eye as a whole can perform its function well.

Health and illness deal with the essential functions of the body, so we cannot avoid seeing that bad health is, in fact, bad. If you have asthma and cannot breathe, if you are blind and cannot see, if you break a leg and cannot walk, it is very obvious that something is wrong.

Some health practitioners go a step beyond essential functioning of the body and say that, instead of just avoiding illness, we should actively promote optimum wellness. We should eat the good diet, do the intense exercise, and live the healthy life that will allow us to achieve optimum physical functioning.

Natural ethics goes another step beyond this and says that we should try to achieve not just wellness but arete, not just the excellent functioning of our physical capabilities but the excellent functioning of all our capabilities – for example, our intelligence, our musical ability, and our moral capability.

Whether we are talking only about health or more broadly about arete, we know what is good and what is bad in the same way.

We begin by knowing intuitively that certain conditions are good or bad. For example, it is good to see clearly and bad to be blind, good to have strong lungs and bad to have asthma, good to be intelligent and bad to be stupid, good to be graceful and bad to be clumsy. These are things we know directly, in the same way that we know the axioms of geometry. They are self-evident in the sense that everyone who is rational can see that they are true. They are self-evident, even though people whose feelings are twisted by emotion and self-interest may deny they are true, as when someone who is stupid spitefully says that it is worthless to be intelligent.

We go on to develop a more general theory based on all these individual judgments, when we see that they all involve capabilities with natural ends. We see that, in every case, it is good for the capability to function well, and that it functions well by achieving its natural end. The function of the eye is to see, and that is why it is good to see clearly and bad to be blind. One function of the intellect is to understand, and that is why it is good to be intelligent and bad to be stupid. This general theory is self-evident, not only in the sense that all rational people can see it is true but also in the sense that it would be self-contradictory to deny it by saying that "it is bad for a capability to function well" or by saying that "a capability is functioning well if it does not achieve its natural telos."

Finally, we observe that we can help our own capabilities and the capabilities of others to function well by behaving in certain ways. This behavior is not self-evidently good in the same way that natural goods are. Everyone can see that it is good to be healthy, strong, and so on, but some people do not see that it is good to be temperate and prudent. It also is not self-contradictory to deny that this sort of behavior is good: for example, it is logically possible that if our physiology were different, we could eat and drink indefinitely without gaining weight or becoming drunkards. We learn that this sort of behavior is good from experience, not from reason.

If we are talking only about promoting health, we call this sort of behavior "a healthy lifestyle." If we are talking more broadly about promoting arete, we call this sort of behavior virtue.

# Self-Evident But Not Universal

If basic principles of natural ethics are so clear, why do different societies have radically different moral codes? Moral relativists claim that the different moralities of different societies show that there is no self-evident morality.

The Greeks who first developed natural ethics knew that different nations had radically different customs. Contact with other nations with radically different customs led the sophists to become moral relativists, led Socrates to search for ethics that is known by reason and independent of the customs of any country, and led some post-Socratic philosophers to develop natural ethics.

The idea that all the nations should know the principles of natural ethics is a later confusion. The Romans tended to identify the Law of Nature, known by reason, with the Law of Nations, which they used to govern all the different peoples in the Roman empire and which they based on common elements in the laws of all these peoples. This idea that all nations had some idea of the natural law was also very influential during the Enlightenment and afterwards.[33]

But this idea was used to undermine natural law theory during the twentieth century, when anthropologists discovered radical differences in values among different cultures and used these differences as an argument for moral relativism. If fundamental moral principles are self-evident, how is it possible that different societies have such different moral systems?

First, if an idea is self-evident, it does not necessarily mean that every society knows it. After you have learned arithmetic and a bit of number theory, it is self-evident that the set of counting numbers is infinite, but this is not self-evident to people who have never learned arithmetic. People did not know this self-evident fact in primitive societies, which often had number systems that did not allow them to count higher than five. Many people living today do not know this self-evident fact, because they have not taken any time to think about it. If you make the effort to understand it, it is self-evident, but primitive societies and many people today have not made that effort. Likewise, primitive societies have never thought about whether there is a natural ethics that transcends their social conventions, and most people today do not think about this question.

Second, there are there are sharp moral differences among societies because their moral codes are distorted by economic necessity and by self-interest.

People can fail to see the self-evident when it is contrary to their interest. When little children divide a large pile of candy by counting the pieces, they usually end up arguing about whether someone got more than his share, and they might count and recount repeatedly without ever agreeing on whether the piles are equal. This does not mean that there is no correct method of counting. It means that the children's selfishness gets in the way of their counting correctly.

When it comes to ethical theory, most people are not much different from those children. Even without thinking about it, most people, do see that natural goods are good: in every society, primitive or civilized, most people believe that it is good to be healthy and bad to be sick, good to be strong and bad to be weak, good to be musically talented and bad to be tone-deaf, good to be graceful and bad to be clumsy. But self-interest leads people with power to want these natural goods for themselves and for those whom they pass their power on to, but not for their inferiors. They want their sons to be strong and intelligent, but do not want the same goods for their daughters, their peasants, or their slaves. They see that these natural goods are good, but like the children dividing candy, they want to get the largest share for themselves.

Most people and most societies have never thought about whether there is a general ethical theory that transcends their society's conventional values and their own self-interest, so they do not recognize the self-evident.

# A Note on Casuistry

Moral principles that are clearly true may be hard to implement in practice. For example, your wages may be so low that, if you take time to exercise, you will not be able to work long enough hours to buy adequate food for yourself, so that there is a conflict between two natural goods (increasing your strength by exercising and staying healthy by eating an adequate diet). Or you may try to feed the hungry in time of famine but find there is not enough food for everyone.

Sometimes, you can decide fairly easily that one course of action is preferable. It is obviously better to buy food and do without exercise than it is to exercise and slowly starve to death. In other cases, it is difficult to see which natural good is more important: most of us would not want to be the one to decide which hungry people are fed and which starve.

We must make difficult decisions when we apply moral principles in real life, but these practical problems do not invalidate the moral principles. It is good to eat a healthy diet, and it is good to exercise, even if some people do not have time to do both. It is good to feed the hungry, even if there sometimes is not enough food for everyone.

Traditionally, the branch of philosophy that dealt with moral principles was called ethics, and the branch that applied these principles in practice was called casuistry. Casuistry is so difficult that the word has come to mean drawn out, fruitless argument, but the difficulty of applying moral principles to practical cases does not invalidate those moral principles.

# Chapter 9

# Ethics and Society

Historically, ethical theory has changed as the needs of society have changed.

In classical Greece, male aristocrats had a great deal of freedom to manage their own lives and to participate in managing the government. As a result, they invented ethical theories based on the idea of arete, which let them use this freedom to develop their humanity fully. But because there was a scarcity economy at the time, only a small minority of all people could have the freedom to try to live fully human lives.

During the industrial revolution, it was necessary to remove traditional restraints that got in the way of economic modernization. Classical natural law ethics was one of these restraints. The idea that nature was nothing more than matter in motion, with no ends of its own, allowed the industrial economy to exploit natural resources and labor, promoting rapid economic growth.

Now, in the developed nations, economic growth has reached the point where most people have enough to live good lives. At the same time, uncontrolled technology and economic growth have become a threat to the world's environment. To help ward off this threat, we need to revive classical natural ethics, which could help us use our technology and our economy as means to live fully human lives.

## Classical Ethics

Primitive societies fall into ethical systems by a sort of natural selection. Economic constraints are tight. A society survives if it adopts roles for men and women that let it subsist economically and if it adopts beliefs and rituals that hold it together socially. Once they fall into these roles and rituals, primitive societies follow them for generation after generation, as long as they continue to allow the society to survive, and as long as there are no new methods of production that demand different roles.

With the rise of civilization, there is some loosening of economic constraint. Classical western ethical theory began in Greece, where there was a class of independent aristocrats, who were wealthy enough to be free from most economic pressures, who managed their own estates, and who governed their own cities. Because these people controlled their own lives, they had reason to think about what is a good life.

Yet in ancient Greece and Rome, the economy had developed to the point where only male aristocrats were free to manage their own lives. When they reasoned about the good life, the moral theories they developed were distorted by their interest in defending their privileges, so they believed that slavery and subordination of women were natural.

# Modernist Ethics

Beginning in the seventeenth century, the industrial revolution introduced a new set of economic constraints. Traditional agricultural economies – and the traditional values and forms of government that went with them – stood in the way of the sustained economic growth that new technology and the accumulation of capital were making possible for the first time. For example, tolls collected at the boundaries of each feudal domain got in the way of trade, and the people's traditional right to use the commons for subsistence got in the way of agricultural production for a larger market.

In this situation, as we would expect, traditional values and the traditional view of the world were swept away in the name of progress. The new physics led philosophers to reject traditional beliefs about the nature of the universe and our place in the universe, and to try to develop modern ethics based on the new science.

Modernist ethics accommodated the new potential for economic growth. Hobbes said explicitly that, unlike classical ethics, a modern ethics based on appetites and aversions implies that there is no limit to human desires:

…the Felicity of this life, consisteth not in the repose of a mind satisfied. For there is no such *Finis ultimus* (utmost ayme,) nor *Summum Bonum* (greatest Good,) as is spoken of in the books of the old Morall Philosophers. ... Felicity is a continuall progress of the desire, from one object to another....[34]

Hobbes' ethics, based on appetites and aversions, and the utilitarians' ethics, based on maximizing gratification, helped to justify the growing capitalist economy. There are endless desires to gratify.

In addition, Hobbes' view that nature is nothing but different combinations of the sort of matter analyzed by the physicists implies that we can manipulate living animals and plants just as we manipulate non-living matter. It turns nature into natural resources, ultimately leading to our efficient industrial farming that uses high inputs of pesticides and herbicides, and that keeps animals confined in small pens from the time they are born until the time they are slaughtered – farming with no respect for nature. At the extreme, this view also turns humans into human resources, who can be manipulated with no respect for their nature.

This sort of modernist ethics, with its scope for endless growth and progress, remained influential through the twentieth century.

Even more strongly than Hobbes, John Dewey criticized the Greeks for coming up with a notion of the good life that could limit progress. The Greeks tried to replace traditional morality with morality based on reasoning about the good life, but, Dewey said, "reason as a substitute for custom was under the obligation of supplying objects and laws as fixed as those of custom had been."[35] Dewey rejected these fixed ends, claiming that "Moral goods and ends exist only when something has to be done,"[36] so that ethics should be redefined as practical work to solve problems:

...experimental logic when carried into morals makes every quality that is judged to be good according as it contributes to amelioration of existing ills. ... When physics, chemistry, biology, medicine, contribute to the detection of concrete human woes and to the development of plans for remedying them, they become moral; they become part of the apparatus of moral inquiry of science. ... Natural science ... becomes in itself humanistic in quality. It is something to be pursued not in a technical and specialized way for what is called truth for its own sake, but with the sense of its social bearing. ... It is technical only in the sense that it provides the technique of social and moral engineering.[37]

Thus, Dewey concludes, "Reason, always an honorific term in ethics, becomes actualized in the methods by which ... intelligent plans of improvement are worked out."[38] But reason can say nothing about the purpose of these improvements, about whether they are directed at a worthwhile end: "the process of growth, improvement and progress, rather than the static outcome and result, becomes the significant thing. ... Growth itself is the only moral 'end.'"[39]

Dewey is expressing the twentieth century's tendency to throw away any limits to progress and to build its way out of every problem. "Fixed ends" would get in the way of endless "growth, improvement and progress."

This approach made some sense at a time when economic scarcity was our central problem, since you can build your way out of scarcity, but it no longer makes sense today.

# After Modernism

Our economic situation has changed dramatically since modernist philosophers rejected classical ethics. Between the seventeenth and early twentieth centuries, it was necessary to get rid of political structures and ethical theories that limited economic growth. But today, we are reaching a point where people in the developed nations have enough economically, so growth no longer offers the critical benefits that it did when people were struggling to produce essentials. At the same time, economic growth has become a threat to the global environment, and technology threatens to reengineer nature and human nature.

We have reached a point where we need an idea of the good life that lets us make good use of our economic prosperity and our technology.

Moral philosophy has become much more important than it was throughout history. Before the twentieth century, most people worked long hours to produce basic food, clothing and shelter for themselves. They did not need moral philosophy to tell them that they should do what they had to do to survive, and it did not make much difference whether they believed in natural ethics or in, say, hedonism, since they would have spent their lives producing necessities for themselves in either case.

Throughout history, only a small leisure class had the luxury of thinking about what was a good life and the means to try to live that good life. But today, in the developed countries, society as a whole has moved beyond scarcity, giving us all the opportunity to try to live a good life.

We can see that our view of the good life makes an immense difference to society, by considering how different the future would be with the three different views of the good life that are most likely to become widespread in the coming century. We could continue the moral drift of recent decades, letting the economy run for its own sake, without being directed by any clear idea of the good life. We could adopt hedonism and consider pleasure central to the good life. Or we could adopt natural ethics and consider developing our capabilities to be central to the good life.

## Moral Drift

During the twentieth century, America moved from a scarcity economy to a surplus economy, but there was no national discussion of how we could use the "high standard of living" to live well, and so we drifted aimlessly, without any idea of the good life to set the direction of the economy. Post-war America maximized economic growth without thinking about the human purposes of growth, as if we were following Dewey's advice that "the process of growth, improvement and progress, rather than the static outcome and result, become the significant thing. ... Growth itself is the only moral 'end.'"[40]

During the flush of post-war prosperity, some intellectuals criticized the empty consumerism of the "affluent society," but these intellectuals did not affect the direction of the economy. Instead of using the economy for human purposes, we manipulated people to fit them into the consumer economy, through advertising and through government policies that promote economic growth. As a result, year after year, we have driven our cars more and more, we have moved to more and more remote suburbs, we have bought bigger and bigger houses, we have bought more and bigger televisions, and so on.

This consumerism was supposed to be "good for the economy" – but very few people claimed that this consumerism added up to a good life. In fact, economists who have studied American's self-reported happiness have found that economic growth does not make us feel that we are better off. Americans are no happier today than they were when they earned half as much as they do now.[41]

Presumably, this sort of drift could continue: we could promote economic growth for the sake of economic growth, without thinking about whether growth increases our happiness.

Our combination of economic growth and moral drift grows out of our inability to have a public discussion of the good life. Our economists believe in the moral philosophy called "preference utilitarianism" (though they may not know the name that philosophers give to their theory). Their theory is based on the idea that we can maximize total satisfaction by allowing individuals to buy the products that give them the most satisfaction, assuming that individuals are the best judges of what they want. Early utilitarians believed that you could determine scientifically what gave people the most pleasure, while today's economists, as preference utilitarians, believe that we must rely on each individual's subjective preference. American conservatives often attack the left for promoting moral relativism, but they do not mention that the capitalist economy they support is also based theoretically on moral relativism.

Today, the only political faction that believes in moral absolutes is made up of religious fundamentalists who base ethics on revelation and not on reason. Society as a whole drifts because we do not have a reasoned public discussion of the good life. Conservatives argue for a capitalist economy based on personal choice, and liberals say that everyone has the right to make decisions about their own lifestyle based on personal choice.

Of course, people should make these personal choices for themselves, but relativistic moral theories do not give people any guidance that will help them make wise choices.

Today, technologies such as genetic engineering and mood-enhancing "designer drugs" threaten to manipulate people far more dramatically than we have ever been manipulated in the past, to change what it means to be human. It is dangerous to continue our usual policy of moral drift, of letting the economy and technology develop in their own terms rather than harnessing them to some idea of the good life.

If we do move beyond our current moral drift, hedonism and natural ethics are probably the two views of the good life that could become widespread enough to becoming guiding principles of our society. These different moral philosophies would lead us to very different futures.

## Hedonism

There are already some hints of what the future might look like if we adopt the hedonists' view of the good life: look at the luxury spas where people go to the steam room, then to an eighty-minute Swedish massage, and then to a gourmet organic luncheon laid out on the terrace, or look at Las Vegas, where people spend their time in fantasy casinos, gambling, eating large meals, watching stage shows, and doing the other things that people do in a city whose motto is "What happens in Las Vegas stays in Las Vegas."

But this is only the beginning. If we were genuinely committed to hedonism, we would look forward to a future where we use designer drugs to give ourselves pleasure without harmful side-effects, or where we use electrodes to directly stimulate the pleasure centers of the brain.

As early as 1954, psychologists James Olds and Peter Milner accidentally placed an electrode in a rat's pleasure center, in the limbic system, while they were doing research on rats brains. Then they performed experiments where a rat could press a lever and stimulate its brain's pleasure center directly, and rats pressed the lever as many as 5,000 times an hour. If they were allowed to, the rats continued to press the lever indefinitely rather than eating, until they died of starvation.

This study led to later research about serotonin and dopamine, and the endorphins, the chemicals in the brain that are associated with pleasure. Psychiatric drugs such as Prozac regulate the level of these chemicals in the brain. Street drugs such as cocaine and ecstasy apparently also affect the pleasure center of the brain, but they have harmful side-effects. In a society devoted to hedonism, there would be research to create drugs that provide the same sort of intense pleasure without side-effects.

These new technologies refute the old philosophy of hedonism. The life with the most pleasure would be a life attached to a machine that gives constant direct stimulation to the pleasure center of your brain, with intravenous feeding and medical care to insure that you live as long as possible. This would give you maximum quantity of pleasure possible in one human life, but no one would call it a good life.

In the past, some philosophers were able to believe in hedonism only because they took for granted that all pleasures were the side-effect of some natural function, such as eating, friendship, sex, or learning. Once we see that it is possible to have pleasure detached from any natural function, by stimulating the brain with electrodes, then it becomes absolutely clear that pleasure itself is not the essence of the good life.

Today, technology is reaching the point where it can bypass natural functioning and provide us with effortless pleasure. The philosophy of hedonism would lead us to the sort of society that Aldous Huxley envisioned in *Brave New World*, where people are genetically engineered to meet the modest demands of the economy with little effort, and where they are kept happy with sex, jazz, consumerism, and drugs. We could add one more thing to Huxley's vision: direct stimulation of the pleasure center of the brain.

## Natural Ethics

The most likely alternative to moral drift or hedonism is natural ethics: the idea that we live a good life by developing and using our natural capabilities as fully as possible.

Let's look at the sort of future that natural ethics could bring by humanizing the economy, by humanizing technology, and by promoting respect for nature.

For one thing, natural ethics would lead us to treat human development as an end and the economy as a means.

This would mean rejecting consumerism and living a bit more simply than we do now, since developing our talents generally requires a relatively moderate outlay of money and a large outlay of time. For example, to develop your musical talent, you might buy a musical instrument and spend long hours practicing on it; to develop yourself physically, you might buy athletic equipment and spend long hours exercising. We would spend money on gymnasiums, concert halls, musical instruments, art and craft studios, libraries, and the like; but we would also be eager to cut back on our work hours and our consumption, so we have more time to exercise, make music, make art, and the like.

For most of the twentieth century, we have considered economic growth good in itself. Instead, we would want economic growth only to the extent that the economy helps us to live well. We would remember what Aristotle said about the natural limits of acquisitiveness:

> One form of property-getting, namely getting a livelihood, is in accordance with nature ... For the amount of property of this kind which would give financial independence adequate for a good life is not limitless .... Wealth is a tool, and there are limits to its uses as to the tools of any craft; both in size and in number there are limits of usefulness ... but there is another kind of property-getting, to which the term money-making is generally and quite rightly applied; and it is due to this that there is thought to be no limit to wealth or acquisition .... Indeed, wealth is often regarded as consisting in a pile of money, since the aim of money-making and of trade is to make such a pile .... In this kind of money-making, in which coined money is both the end pursued in the transaction and the medium by which the transaction is performed, there is no limit to the amount of riches to be got.[42]

Our economists tell us that, the larger the Gross Domestic Product is, the better off we are; they believe that wealth consists of a pile of money. If we had an ethical theory that centered on human nature, like Aristotle's, we would see that economic growth has a natural limit: the economy should grow to the point where it allows us develop our natural capabilities as fully as possible.

An ethical theory that centers on nature would also tell us that we should avoid technologies that change our nature, such as mood altering drugs and germ-line genetic engineering.

Genetic engineering opens up a moral abyss. In the past, when we bred plants and domestic animals to suit human purposes – for example, cows that give more milk, grasses that produce more grain, and dogs that herd sheep – even while they were bred for these purposes, the living things always had their own natures that deserved respect. As people domesticated cows, for example, it was always true that they should not treat them cruelly, that they should let them graze rather than keeping them in a pen for life, and so on. But in the future, it is conceivable that we can genetically engineer cows so that they are designed to live in pens: we could conceivably create cows that cannot walk, that take pleasure in being cramped in tiny pens, and that hate to be let out. If we redesign animals' natures solely to serve our ends, it is meaningless to say that we should have respect for their natures rather than treating them solely as means to our own ends, because they have no natures apart from the ones we give them to suit our own ends.

And if we redesign human nature, it is meaningless to say that there is any such thing as a good life in accordance with human nature. At the time when we are deciding how to genetically engineer a species, animal or human, we are completely outside of and above morality. That is what people mean when they say that genetic engineering is wrong because "we shouldn't play God."

Modern technology can to give everyone the opportunity to live a good life: in classical times, only aristocrats had adequate income and adequate leisure to develop their human capabilities fully, but modernization has made our economy so productive that now everyone can have the income and leisure to live a fully human and good life. But modern technology can also change nature and human nature so drastically that it creates a moral void and makes the idea of the good life meaningless.

## *Respect for Nature*

An ethical theory based on nature would change our attitude toward nature as a whole, as well as our attitude toward our own nature.

Natural ethics applies more broadly than other schools of ethics. Kant said that we should treat all people as ends in themselves rather than just as means to our own ends, but because he based ethics on reason, he applied this principle only to other people, to beings who are capable of reasoning.

Utilitarians based ethics on pleasure and pain, so they often apply a similar principle to animals as well as people: we should maximize pleasure and minimize pain of all creatures that are capable of feeling pleasure and pain. Natural ethics is based on natural capabilities functioning well, so it should apply a similar principle to all living things: people, animals, and plants all have natural teleology that we should respect.

Natural ethics implies that we should treat all living things as ends in themselves, rather than just as means to our ends.

We should preserve and restore wilderness, particularly the ecosystems that are teeming with the most life. We should try to bring ecosystems to the climax state where they contain the greatest abundance and diversity of life, though we should be very careful about interventions that we undertake to strengthen ecosystems, because there is always a danger that we may cause unexpected damage. Natural ecosystems do not let most living things develop fully – most seedlings die rather than growing into trees, predators kill young animals before they mature, populations die back because of famine, and so on – but preserving these ecosystems does create the greatest abundance and diversity of life that is possible.

On cultivated land, we should avoid monoculture, pesticides, and herbicides, to keep the land healthy and let wildlife thrive, rather than using the land solely for our own purposes of producing food. Likewise, we should raise livestock by letting the animals graze in the open fields, rather than forcing them to live their entire lives in pens where they can hardly move.

It is wrong to confine animals in these small pens, because it does not let the animals develop natural capabilities, such as the ability to walk. Despite Kant, it is wrong even though the farm animals are not rational. Despite the utilitarians, it would be wrong even if we made it pleasurable for the animals – for example, by directly stimulating the pleasure centers of their brains.

We have to kill living things in order to eat, but we should, as much as possible, treat the plants and animals we raise for food in a way that respects their own natures.

# The Need For Philosophy

Modernist ethics unsettled traditional values at a time when this was necessary to promote modernization and overcome scarcity. But modernist ethics does not provide what we need today to make good use of the prosperity that modernization can bring.

Today's dominant ethical theories, the right's preference utilitarianism and the left's moral relativism, cannot tell us when consumerism has gone too far: they cannot find anything wrong with teenagers who want $200 jogging shoes, or suburbanites who want McMansions and two sports utility vehicles. Our capitalist economists, as preference utilitarians, would say that these people are right to maximize the satisfaction they get from consuming. Our leftist social critics, as moral relativists would say (if they were consistent) that these people are making a "lifestyle choice" that is as valid as any other.

Likewise, today's dominant ethical theories cannot give us a reason to reject genetic engineering, designer drugs, and other technologies that could lead us to a post-human future. Preference utilitarians would say that individuals should be free to choose these technologies in order to maximize the satisfaction they get from consuming. Moral relativists would say that these technologies might offend people with certain value systems, but would not offend people with other value systems.

To make good use of the modern economy, we need an idea of the good life that transcends arbitrary choice. To choose technologies wisely, we need an ethics that lets us select technologies that do not deface nature or human nature. To move beyond purposeless economic growth, we need an ethics that lets us say we have reached a point where we have enough.

Fortunately, it is not hard to move beyond modernist ethical theories, because they were based on a faith in science and progress that is no longer convincing. In the seventeenth century, new discoveries in physics were so impressive that it seemed they would let us understand the universe completely, from the motion of the planets, to animal behavior, to human emotions. Philosophers tried and failed to develop an ethical theory based on this "scientific" view of the world.

We need to see through this sort of scientism and take a more modest view of what the sciences tell us: the sciences explain their own subject matters but do not explain everything. Once we move beyond scientism, we will be able to revive natural ethics, which could let us make good use of our modern economy and technology.

Initially, moral philosophy was only important to a few aristocrats who had the leisure and means to try to live a good life, but now it is needed to humanize our economy and our technology. If we continue to drift morally, or if we adopt the philosophy of hedonism, we will move toward a post-human future. If we adopt the philosophy of natural ethics, we could move toward a future where, for the first time in history, most people will be have the opportunity to develop their humanity fully.

# Notes

[1] "Letter from a Birmingham Jail" in Martin Luther King, Jr., *Why We Can't Wait* (New York, New American Library: Signet Books, 1964) p. 82.

[2] David Hume, *A Treatise of Human Nature*, Book 3, Part 1, Section 1.

[3] Aristotle, *Politics*, I, 2, trans. T.A. Sinclair.

[4] Aristotle, *Nicomachaen Ethics*, I, 7, trans. David Ross.

[5] Aristotle, *Nichomachean Ethics*, X, 7.

[6] For an overview of stoic ethics and collections of relevant fragments, see A.A. Long and D.N. Sedley, *The Hellenistic Philosophers*, (Cambridge and New York, Cambridge University Press, 1987) pp. 344-437.

[7] See Seneca, *Of Providence.*

[8] Thomas Aquinas, *Summa Theologica*, Part I, Question 80, Article 1.

[9] Dante, *Purgatorio*, canto xviii, lines 28-33, trans. John Ciardi.

[10] Aquinas, *Summa Theologica*, Part I, Question 81, Article 3.

[11] Alasdair MacIntyre, *After Virtue* (Notre Dame, Indiana, University of Notre Dame Press, 1981).

[12] Introduction by C.B. Macpherson, Thomas Hobbes, *Leviathan* (Harmondsworth, Middlesex, England and New York, Penguin, 1951) p. 19.

[13] One failing of this sort of pure social contract theory is not often mentioned. Because there is no moral obligation until there is a contract, people in the state of nature have a right to do anything that advances their self-interest. So, when Europeans colonized the world, they had no natural moral obligation to the people they found: they could form a social contract with these people, or they could conquer and enslave them – whichever they thought was in their own best interest. Likewise, there is no moral obligation to animals, because we cannot contract with them.

[14] Hobbes, *Leviathan*, Part I, Chapter 15.

[15] Hobbes, *Leviathan*, Part I, Chapter 15.

[16] Hume, *Treatise of Human Nature*, Book 2, Part 3, Section 3.

[17] David Hume, *An Enquiry Concerning the Principles of Morals*, Section IX, Part 1.

[18] Hume, *An Enquiry Concerning the Principles of Morals*, Section IX, Part 2.

[19] Hume, *An Enquiry Concerning Human Understanding*, Section VIII, Part 1.

[20] Ruth Benedict, *Patterns of Culture* (New York, Mentor Books, 1946).

[21] Friedrich Nietzsche, *Twilight of the Idols*, Maxim 12, trans. Walter Kaufmann.

[22] Alfred Jules Ayer, *Language, Truth and Logic* ((New York, Dover, 1952).

[23] R.M. Hare, *The Language of Morals* (Oxford, Clarendon Press, Oxford University Paperback, 1964, first published 1952) pp. 153-155.

[24] Today, some anthropologists are claiming that there is a common moral sense that evolved because groups where people cooperate are more likely to survive. It almost seems that they are atoning for the sins of Ruth Benedict by going back to the theory of Hume. But they are no more able than Hume was to answer the question of why we should follow this moral sense rather than following our self-interested impulses, which also evolved for good Darwinian reasons. In fact, they are worse off than Hume, because there are obvious Darwinian reasons that we evolved to cooperate within our own tribe but to exterminate other competing tribes; evolutionary psychology gives us no reason for saying that our impulse to cooperate within our own group is moral while our impulse to commit genocide against other groups is immoral. These anthropologists give us interesting insights into how the moral sense evolved historically, but no insight at all into how the moral sense can be justified logically, and as a result, they have had little or no influence on philosophy. For an example of this sort of anthropological argument, see Frans de Waal, *Good Natured: The Origins of Right and Wrong in Humans and Other Animals* (Cambridge, Mass, Harvard University Press, 1996) and Frans de Waal *et al.*, *Primates and Philosophers: How Morality Evolved* (Princeton, NJ, Princeton University Press, 2006). The latter book includes essays by several philosophers, which point out the limits of the anthropologist's approach.

[25] Immanuel Kant, *Prolegomena to Any Future Metaphysics*, Kant's introduction.

[26] Immanuel Kant, *Groundwork of the Metaphysics of Morals*, ch. 2, trans. H.J. Patton (NY, Harper Torchbooks, 1964), p. 89

[27] John Maynard Keynes "My Early Beliefs,' excerpted in Herbert Kohl, *The Age of Complexity* (New York, Mentor Books, 1965) p. 55.

[28] As quoted previously, Hume, *Treatise of Human Nature*, Book 3, Part 1, Section 1.

[29] These quotations are from Aristotle, *The Motion of Animals*, VII, 701a, 10-35. Aristotle also discusses practical syllogisms in *Nichomachean Ethics*, VI, 12.

[30] In addition to new ideas about the good life that appear when people discover new natural capabilities, such as the ability to read, there are also new ideas about the good life that appear when people discover new means to actualize our natural capabilities – new instrumental knowledge, rather than new knowledge

about ends. Our ideas about the virtues and vices can change because of empirical findings that are instrumental, new findings about means, as well as because of new empirical findings about ends. For example, people always knew that gluttony was a vice, because they could always see that eating too much damaged health. But now we have learned more about nutrition, and we know not only that it is unhealthy to eat too much but also that it is unhealthy to eat refined sugar, saturated fat, and other junk food. We know that eating a diet made up entirely of candy bars and Coca Cola will damage your health, even if you eat a moderate amount and are not a glutton in the usual sense. Likewise, people always knew that habitual drunkenness was a vice; once methamphetemines were discovered, it became equally obvious that being addicted to them is a vice; being an addict dulls your mind and your judgment, like being a drunk.

[31] Pierre-Simon Laplace, *Philosophical Essays on Probability* (New York: Springer-Verlag, 1995).

[32] Jean-Paul Sartre, *Existentialism Is a Humanism*, Carol Macomber trans. (New Haven, Connecticut, Yale University Press, 2007).

[33] For example, Montesqueue's *Persian Letters* is typical of many enlightenment satires that criticize corrupt European ethics by exposing them to the gaze of someone from another country, who has a more natural moral code, closer to the universal dictates of natural law. For a twentieth century book that makes the same assumption that natural law must be universal, see C.S. Lewis, *The Abolition of Man*.(New York, Collier Books, 1962).

[34] Hobbes, *Leviathan*, Part I, Chapter xi.

[35] John Dewey, *Reconstruction in Philosophy* (New York, New American Library: Mentor Books, 1950) p. 131.

[36] Dewey, *Reconstruction in Philosophy*, p. 136

[37] Dewey, *Reconstruction in Philosophy*, p. 138 -139.

[38] Dewey, *Reconstruction in Philosophy*, p. 140.

[39] Dewey, *Reconstruction in Philosophy*, p. 141.

[40] Dewey, *Reconstruction in Philosophy*, p. 141.

[41] The research is summarized in James Gustave Speth, *The Bridge at the End of the World: Capitalism, the Environment, and Crossing from Crisis to Sustainability* (New Haven and London, Yale University Press, 2008) p. 129 *et seq.*

[42] Aristotle, *Politics*, I, 9-10.